BRAIN GAMES

MYSTERY PUZZLES

Unsolved crimes, secret
codes, whodunits, and more

pil

Publications International, Ltd.

Additional images from Shutterstock.com

Brain Games is a registered trademark of Publications International, Ltd.

Louis Weber, CEO
Publications International, Ltd.
8140 Lehigh Avenue
Morton Grove, IL 60053

Permission is never granted for commercial purposes.

ISBN: 978-1-63938-019-0

Manufactured in U.S.A.

8 7 6 5 4 3 2 1

Let's get social!

@Publications_International

@PublicationsInternational

@BrainGames.TM

www.pilbooks.com

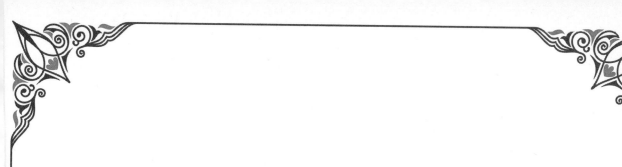

Mystery Is on the Menu

Do you have a fan fiction manuscript of *Z is for Zero* hiding on your laptop?
Do you stay up past midnight to be the first to stream the hottest new crime
series? Then this is your chance to hone your sleuthing skills.

Brain Games® Mystery Puzzles features an assortment of nearly 300 puzzles
created to engage your senses. Visual puzzles to train your eyes to spot small
details, memory puzzles to sharpen your focus, logic puzzles to enhance your
reasoning skills, and much more.

This collection also includes puzzle institutions like: crime-themed word
searches, crosswords, and mazes. Some puzzle solutions will likely come
to you faster than others. If you get stuck along the way, a full answer key is
provided at the back of the book.

All that's left to do now is turn the page to start your investigation!

Finding a Mole

Be a superspy and track down the mole! Change just one letter on each line to go from the top word to the bottom word. Do not change the order of the letters. You must have a common English word at each step.

FIND

MIND

MINE

MILE

MOLE

Tell a Tale, Go to Jail

Change just one letter on each line to go from the top word to the bottom word. Do not change the order of the letters. You must have a common English word at each step.

TALE

TALL

PALL

PAIL

JAIL

Answers on page 348.

Interception

You've intercepted a message that is meant to reveal a location for an upcoming meeting between two criminal masterminds. The only problem is, the message shows many place names. Can you figure out the right location?

RABAT

GHENT

YAREN

MALTA

QUITO

TUNIS

The Suspect's Escape Route

This professional building is a maze of corridors and cubicles. Elevators are local or express only; there are no stairs. And over-stressed office workers won't give you directions to the exit. Can you track the suspect before they escape to their waiting cab?

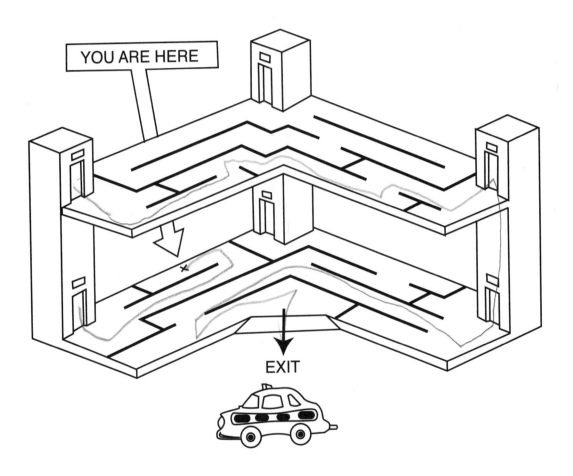

Answer on page 348.

Crime Anagrams

Unscramble each word or phrase below to reveal a word or phrase of a crime.

DANK PIPING

BARBERRY DOME

CHAT FRET

AGATE SOB

ROTE TOXIN

ECZEMA GRIDIRON

KIT GRUFF CARDING

MOBBING

Answers on page 348.

Women of Mystery

ACROSS

1. Watch pocket
4. Likely
7. _____ point (center of activity)
12. Eisenhower's nickname
13. Caviar, e.g.
14. Black
15. Writer Sue of the Kinsey Millhone alphabet mysteries
17. Greene of "Bonanza"
18. H.H. Munro's nom de plume
19. Arrive at the curb
21. In that place
23. Thwack a fly
26. Dell alternative
29. Genesis garden
30. Actress Garr
31. Actor Hawke
33. Singer K.T. _____
34. Ripped
35. Razor choice
38. Set down

39. Heroic tale
40. Egyptian capital
42. "Button your lip!"
44. Page
48. Preminger and Kruger
50. Writer Ruth whose "A Dark-Adapted Eye" won the '87 Edgar
52. Gullible
53. "Born in the _____"
54. Herbert Hoover's First Lady
55. Complies
56. Farm enclosure
57. Perceive

DOWN

1. Newton fruits
2. Gumbo veggie
3. Bird's bill
4. MoMA display
5. All tuckered out
6. Secure faculty status
7. Plummeted
8. Certain woodwind musicians

9. Crime novelist Patricia who writes the Dr. Kay Scarpetta series
10. Legendary advice columnist Landers
11. Soap ingredient
16. Temper tantrum
20. Ex-QB Dawson
22. Fowl female
24. Diva's song
25. Itsy-bitsy
26. Dole (out)
27. On the crest of
28. Author Agatha who created Hercule Poirot and Jane Marple

32. Pizza tidbit
33. Galley propeller
35. Behave
36. Zodiac sign in May
37. Most fully matured
41. On its last legs
43. Brings into play
45. Squirmy catches
46. Burn soother
47. Ventilation duct
48. "Double Fantasy" singer
49. Diet cola introduced in 1963
51. Negative vote

Track the Fugitive

The investigator is tracking the fugitive's past trips in order to find and recover information that was left behind in five cities. Each city was visited only once. Can you put together the travel timeline, using the information below?

1. Indianapolis was not the third city visited.

2. The fugitive went north along the coastline immediately after visiting Las Vegas.

3. Pensacola was neither the first nor last city visited.

4. Montpelier was visited sometime before Indianapolis, but not immediately before.

5. Portland was visited sometime before Pensacola, but not immediately before.

Answer on page 348.

DNA Sequence

Examine the two images below carefully. Are these sequences a match or not?

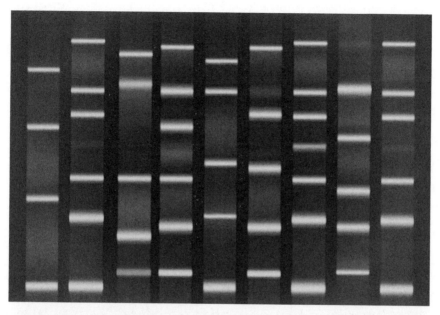

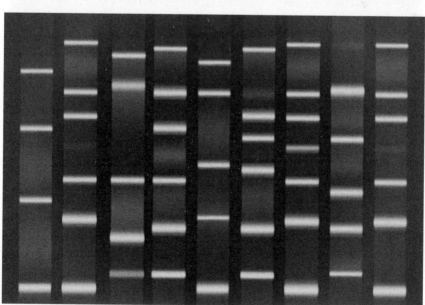

20th Century Mystery Authors

The investigator is tracking the fugitive's past trips in order to find and recover information that was left behind in five cities. Each city was visited only once. Can you put together the travel timeline, using the information below?

CHANDLER (Raymond)

CHILD (Lee)

CHRISTIE (Agatha)

COBEN (Harlan)

CONNELLY (Michael)

CORNWELL (Patricia)

DOYLE (Arthur Conan)

EVANOVICH (Janet)

GRAFTON (Sue)

GRISHAM (John)

HAMMETT (Dashiell)

JAMES (P.D.)

KEENE (Carolyn)

LEHANE (Dennis)

PARKER (Robert B.)

PATTERSON (James)

RASKIN (Ellen)

ROBB (J.D.)

SAYERS (Dorothy)

TUROW (Scott)

```
U Y A C W D W P Z M L M S L K P
B C F L G O G S G B W V F D D E
M O R R R Y R R W A O H F N Z
X B U U A L C E Y R I L L A L E
E E T Q F E M Y L L G S H M I B
N N B N T Y M A L L Z E H T P S
E P O D O Z B S E T L M S A D D
E A F F N S R K N C U I P S M U
K T U A J Y D V N Q R I E R W D
Q T D L I H C O O H J A M E S V
S E V A N O V I C H A N D L E R
T R Z J N V V L O J F G F M J V
I S O L L E W N R O C E G N F X
K O B B O R P A R K E R J N O G
J N J O M Z W G W L N I K S A R
H A M M E T T L K L P O V O E D
```

type

Answers on page 349.

13

Heist of the 21st Century

Cryptograms are messages in substitution code. Break the code to read the message. For example, THE SMART CAT might become FVO QWGDF JGF if **F** is substituted for **T, V** for **H, O** for **E,** and so on.

UQXO UXM MOHDGF AF OQG MH-TXDDGP QGAMO

HK OQG TGFORLY? PAXEHFPM, ILAEXLADY, UAOQ

MHEG NHDP XFP BGUGDLY KHL NHHP EGXMRLG. OQG

OHOXD TXEG OH EHLG OQXF HFG QRFPLGP EADDAHF

PHDDXLM. OQG NHHPM UGLG MOHDGF KLHE OQG

XFOUGLI UHLDP PAXEHFP TGFOLG AF VGDNARE. OQG

OQAGK GMOXVDAMQGP QAEMGDK XM X OGFXFO OH

OQG VRADPAFN, GFXVDAFN QAM XTTGMM OH OQG

SXRDO. QG UXM TXRNQO VXMGP HF X MXFPUATQ

DGKO FGXL OQG TLAEG MTGFG. OQG PAXEHFPM,

QHUGSGL, UGLG FHO LGTHSGLGP.

Answer on page 349.

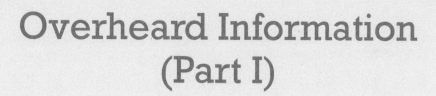

Overheard Information
(Part I)

Read the story below, then turn the page and answer the questions.

Patricia eavesdropped on a suspicious conversation this afternoon while riding home on the bus. One man did all the talking: "I swear to you, George, it'll be the easiest job we've ever done. They close the jewelry store down at 5:00pm, and all staff are out by 5:45pm. The security guard doesn't start his shift until 6:30pm so we'll have plenty of time. The assistant manager already gave me the alarm code – 4781 - in return for a 30% cut, and he promised to leave the engagement ring showcase unlocked on Thursday night. I've already got Steve lined up to drive the getaway car – are you in?"

Overheard Information (Part II)

(Do not read this until you have read the previous page!)

1. What type of store are the men planning to rob?
   A. jewelry store
   B. electronics store
   C. restaurant
   D. hair salon

2. Which of the following numbers is not in the alarm code?
   A. 2
   B. 1
   C. 7
   D. 4

3. How much time will they have to perform the heist between the time the staff leaves the store and the time the security guard shows up for his night shift?
   A. 45 minutes
   B. 15 minutes
   C. 1 hour
   D. 30 minutes

4. How much of a cut is the assistant manager getting in return for handing over the alarm code?
   A. 25%
   B. 15%
   C. 50%
   D. 30%

Answers on page 349.

Seen at the Scene (Part I)

Study this picture of the crime scene for 1 minute, then turn the page.

Seen at the Scene (Part II)

(Do not read this until you have read the previous page!)

1. What furniture did you see in the background?
   A. bookshelf
   B. rocking chair
   C. sofa

2. The investigator is wearing protective booties over shoes.
   _____ True
   _____ False

3. The investigator is photographing this item.
   A. briefcase / satchel
   B. an open book
   C. a woman's small purse

Answers on page 349.

Motel Hideout

A thief hides out in one of the 45 motel rooms listed in the chart below. The motel's in-house detective received a sheet of four clues, signed "The Logical Thief." Using these clues, the detective found the room number within 10 minutes—but by that time, the thief had fled. Can you find the thief's motel room more quickly?

1. When you multiply the digits together, the resulting number is greater than 20.

2. The number is neither a multiple of 7 nor contains the digit 7.

3. The second digit is larger than the first by at least 3.

4. The sum of the digits is less than 12.

51	52	53	54	55	56	57	58	59
41	42	43	44	45	46	47	48	49
31	32	33	34	35	36	37	38	39
21	22	23	24	25	26	27	28	29
11	12	13	14	15	16	17	18	19

Jump on a Train

You're on a runaway train that won't stop moving forward! The path from start to finish must follow the curve of the loops; sharp turns aren't allowed.

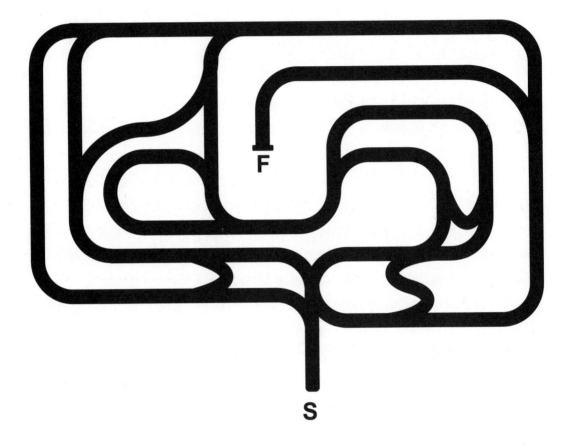

Answer on page 349.

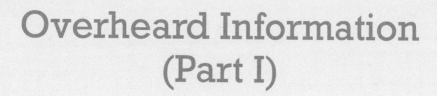

Overheard Information (Part I)

Read the story below, then turn the page and answer the questions.

Sam works as a bartender at a local hotel. It's not unusual for him to overhear some strange conversations from time to time, but last night's was peculiar enough that he felt obligated to share it with the police. A woman in her mid 30s was speaking to an older man: "At 2:00pm on April 13th, have Creed and Paul ready on the corner of Palm Street and Trestle Lane. The armored car driver – Vinnie - will stop there immediately after he picks up the weekly cash deposit from First Surety Bank. He'll get out at the intersection and pretend he's having a heart attack to distract the other guard and get him to unlock the door – that's when your guys will strike. Our man on the inside says to expect at least $3 million in cash. $250k for each of your guys, $500k to the driver – the rest is ours to split 50/50."

Overheard Information
(Part II)

(Do not read this until you have read the previous page!)

1. At what intersection will the armored car heist go down?
   - A. Midland and Fourth
   - B. Prince and Wright
   - C. First and Third
   - D. Palm and Trestle

2. What bank is the armored car stopping at on the day of the heist?
   - A. Capital Trust
   - B. First Surety
   - C. Credit First
   - D. First Financial

3. How much money will be paid to the armored car driver?
   - A. $100,000
   - B. $500,000
   - C. $250,000
   - D. $350,000

4. What are the names of the two robbers?
   - A. Chris and Paul
   - B. Creed and Phil
   - C. Creed and Paul
   - D. Chip and Pat

Answers on page 349.

Track the Fugitive

The investigator is tracking the fugitive's past trips in order to find and recover information that was left behind in five cities. Each city was visited only once. Can you put together the travel timeline, using the information below?

1. From Berlin, the fugitive went directly to the other capital city in Europe.

2. Tokyo was not the last city visited.

3. Santiago was visited sometime before, but not immediately before, Lisbon.

4. Algiers was one of the first three cities visited, but not the first.

5. From Asia, the fugitive went directly to South America.

The Museum Robbery

The Gracklethorpe Museum was robbed last night! The thieves got away with five paintings total. Each piece was by a different painter, and each was stolen from a different room in the museum. No two paintings have the same value (for insurance purposes). Using only the clues below, match each of the missing paintings to its artist and the room from which it was stolen, and determine the replacement value of each.

1. The five paintings were: the one stolen from the Russia Room, Orpheus II, Cape Valley, the one by Ben Binford and the one valued at $250,000.

2. Of May Morning and the $500,000 painting, one was stolen from the Penforth Room and the other was painted by Elsforth Etz during his time in St. Moritz.

3. Ben Binford didn't paint Sea at Night.

4. The Cal Carson painting is twice as expensive as the one by Elsforth Etz.

5. Cape Valley (which wasn't by Debbie Dale) is worth one-eighth as much as the painting that was stolen from the Nixon Room.

6. Orpheus II has always been on display in the Gold Room.

7. May Morning was valued at one million dollars.

		Paintings					Artists					Rooms				
		Blue Elba	Cape Valley	May Morning	Orpheus II	Sea at Night	Alice Ames	Ben Binford	Cal Carson	Debbie Dale	Elsforth Etz	Bayreux	Gold	Nixon	Penforth	Russia
Values	$250,000															
	$500,000															
	$1,000,000															
	$2,000,000															
	$4,000,000															
Rooms	Bayreux															
	Gold															
	Nixon															
	Penforth															
	Russia															
Artists	Alice Ames															
	Ben Binford															
	Cal Carson															
	Debbie Dale															
	Elsforth Etz															

Values	Paintings	Artists	Rooms
$250,000			
$500,000			
$1,000,000			
$2,000,000			
$4,000,000			

Call the Cops

ACROSS

1. Neighborhood cop, e.g.
5. Some luxury cars
8. Hit the sack
9. Slangy way to say "No!"
10. Annoyed state
11. "I Remember You" band
12. Cop, as an authority figure
14. Cop of the highway patrol
17. Uninterpreted info
19. Bible book before Philemon
21. Royal domain
22. Cop who's a detective
23. Used pencils, perhaps
24. Time of low temps

DOWN

1. Get steamy
2. Refinish, perhaps
3. "Animal Farm," e.g.
4. Most peculiar
6. Major responsibility for a parent
7. Draw back
9. Going to the dogs, e.g.
12. Blush
13. Theft deterrent
15. Where meals are made
16. Fluorescent pigment brand
18. Humpback, e.g.
19. Like a wallflower
20. 4-0 World Series win, e.g.

Track the Fugitive

The investigator is tracking the fugitive's past trips in order to find and recover information that was left behind in five cities. Each city was visited only once. Can you put together the travel timeline, using the information below?

1. The visit to Guadalajara came directly between the visits to the two Canadian cities one of which was Vancouver.

2. Helsinki was one of the first two cities visited.

3. Vienna was visited immediately after the other city that began with V.

4. Montreal was visited sometime before Vienna.

Answer on page 350.

DNA Sequence

Examine the two images below carefully. Are these sequences a match or not?

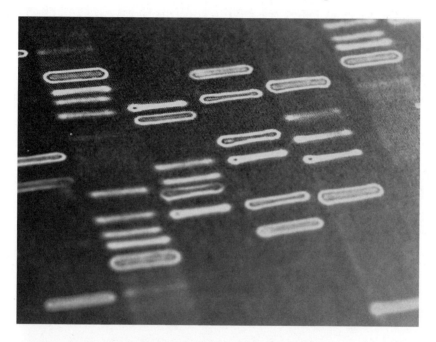

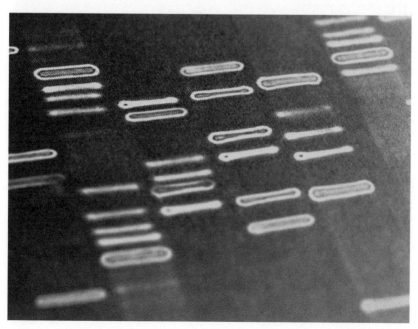

Answer on page 350.

You're Under Arrest

Cryptograms are messages in substitution code. Break the code to read the message. For example, THE SMART CAT might become FVO QWGDF JGF if **F** is substituted for **T, V** for **H, O** for **E,** and so on.

QGT FLKA RFA YCDFR RG YABLCE VCJAER. LEQRFCED

QGT VLQ ULE LEZ PCJJ NA TVAZ LDLCEVR QGT CE

L UGTYR GO JLP. QGT FLKA RFA YCDFR RG LE LRRG-

YEAQ. CO QGT ULEEGR LOOGYZ LE LRRGYEAQ, GEA

PCJJ NA MYGKCZAZ OGY QGT. ZG QGT TEZAYVRLEZ

RFA YCDFRV C FLKA WTVR YALZ RG QGT? PCRF RFAVA

YCDFRV CE BCEZ, ZG QGT PCVF RG VMALX RG BA?

Answer on page 350.

Track the Fugitive

The investigator is tracking the fugitive's past trips in order to find and recover information that was left behind in five cities. Each city was visited only once. Can you put together the travel timeline, using the information below?

1. From Bangkok the fugitive went immediately to Singapore or vice versa.

2. The fugitive did not go to or from the other U.S. city from Chicago.

3. Madrid was visited sometime before Austin, but not immediately before.

4. Chicago was visited sometime before Singapore.

5. Two other cities separated the visit to Madrid and the visit to Singapore.

Answer on page 350.

The Black Dahlia Murder Mystery

Every word listed is contained within the group of letters. Words can be found in a straight line horizontally, vertically, or diagonally. They may be read either forward or backward.

ABRASIONS	HORRIFIC	POLICE
BLACK	IDENTIFICATION	POSED
BLOOD	INVESTIGATION	OFFICERS
BODY	KILLER	REPORTERS
CALIFORNIA	KNIFE	SCENE
CEMENT	LACERATION	STREET
CRIME	LEADS	UNKNOWN
DAHLIA	MURDER	VACANT
FOOTPRINT	NAKED	WEAPON
GHOULISH	NEWSPAPERS	WOMAN
GRISLY	NUMEROUS	

The murder of Elizabeth Short in 1947 gained worldwide fame for its sheer gruesomeness. Short's body was discovered in a vacant lot in the Leimert Park area of Los Angeles. Most horrific was that her body had been completely severed at the midsection, and the two halves had been placed as if they were part of some morbid display. The press gave her the nickname the Black Dahlia. As time wore on, hundreds of police officers were assigned to the Black Dahlia investigation. The case has never been solved.

```
M X V S T R E E T E C I L O P G Z
U S U N K N O W N N O B L O O D U
R R Y Q T G S X D K I L L E R J X
D E D N N Y H B D N F R P X L N F
E T O D O R L O E G O I P O L G T
R R B O I I B S U F D P C T S B S
S O C A T K T P I L I A A U O E X
U P A C A K C A A R I N H E L O D
O E L L C X L I G B G S K L W S F
R R I B I O C M F I R C H T I Y X
E V F L F F E N O I T A R E C A L
M A O A I F M L W S R S S I V K W
U C R C T I E E D O C R E I M H K
N A N K N C N A J U M E O V O E E
K N I W E E T D D E K A N H N N T
S T A H D R B S W J P Z N E U I S
S R X V I S N E W S P A P E R S J
```

Motel Hideout

A thief hides out in one of the 45 motel rooms listed in the chart below. The motel's in-house detective received a sheet of four clues, signed "The Logical Thief." Using these clues, the detective found the room number within 15 minutes—but by that time, the thief had fled. Can you find the thief's motel room more quickly?

1. The number is divisible by 3.

2. The number is not divisible by 6.

3. The first digit is equal to or larger than the second.

4. The sum of the digits is not 6.

51	52	53	54	55	56	57	58	59
41	42	43	44	45	46	47	48	49
31	32	33	34	35	36	37	38	39
21	22	23	24	25	26	27	28	29
11	12	13	14	15	16	17	18	19

Answer on page 351.

Open Conundrums

Cryptograms are messages in substitution code. Break the code to read the message. For example, THE SMART CAT might become FVO QWGDF JGF if **F** is substituted for **T**, **V** for **H**, **O** for **E**, and so on.

RLO CQBX-UZBBMBX BNF GOUMOG "ZBGQCJOE WP-GROUMOG" VUQAMCOE WQUO RLTB 1,300 FUM-WMBTC "WPGROUMOG" QJOU MRG 230-OVMGQEO UZB. TG T UOGZCR, LTCA RLO FTGOG AOTRZUMBX ITBROE AZXMRMJOG LTJO NOOB GQCJOE, WQUO RLTB 100 ATWMCMOG LTJO NOOB UOZBMROE IMRL CQGR CQJOE QBOG, TBE GOJOB MBEMJMEZTCG ILQ IOUO IUQBXCP FQBJMFROE QA FUMWOG, LTJO NOOB OS-QBOUTROE TBE UOCOTGOE.

The Suspect's Escape Route

This professional building is a maze of corridors and cubicles. Elevators are local or express only; there are no stairs. And over-stressed office workers won't give you directions to the exit. Can you track the suspect before they escape to their waiting cab?

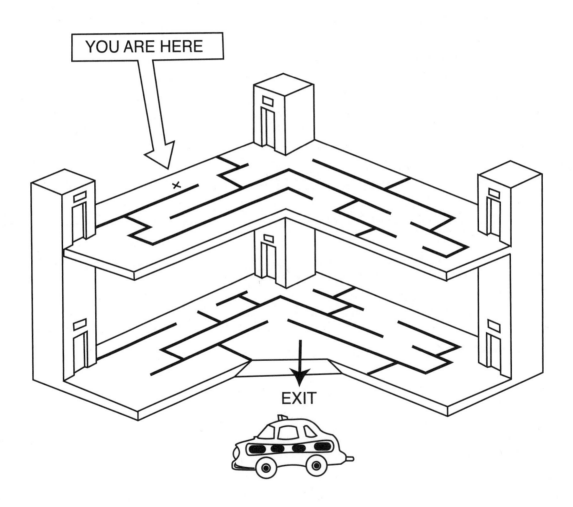

YOU ARE HERE

EXIT

Answer on page 351.

Cold Case

Change just one letter on each line to go from the top word to the bottom word. Do not change the order of the letters. You must have a common English word at each step.

COLD

_____

_____

_____

_____

_____

CASE

First Steal, then Flee

Change just one letter on each line to go from the top word to the bottom word. Do not change the order of the letters. You must have a common English word at each step.

STEAL

_____

_____

_____

_____

FLEES

Answers on page 351.

Crime Anagrams

Unscramble each word or phrase below to reveal a word or phrase related to the Most Wanted list.

I GUT FIVE

ERUPT CAD

ACE MEN

POETIC OFFS

RED HAPPENED

COIFFED FILE

DRAWER

UPROOTS NICE

Answers on page 351.

Overheard Information
(Part I)

Read the story below, then turn the page and answer the questions.

A woman came into Precinct 12 this afternoon to report a suspicious conversation she'd overheard in an alley while taking out her morning trash. A tall man was speaking softly to a short man: "The kidnapping is set for Friday evening. At 6:45pm, Princess Antonia's limousine will pull up in front of her apartment on Park Avenue to take her to the opera. Her usual bodyguard, Paulo, will call in sick that night, and Jake, her driver, is on our payroll. He will pretend there is engine trouble and pull over 10 minutes later under the 45th Street bridge. Rick and Maurice will be waiting there in the Land Rover to grab her. We all circle back to the safe house 30 miles north in Juniper Hills by 8:00pm. Ransom will be $20 million."

Overheard Information (Part II)

(Do not read this until you have read the previous page!)

1. **At approximately what time do the criminals plan to kidnap the princess?**
   A. 6:55pm
   B. 6:30pm
   C. 7:35pm
   D. 8:00pm

2. **What is the name of the limousine driver?**
   A. Paulo
   B. Anthony
   C. Junior
   D. Jake

3. **What type of car will the kidnappers be driving?**
   A. Mercedes
   B. Toyota
   C. BMW
   D. Land Rover

4. **Where will the kidnapping take place?**
   A. In an alley
   B. Under a bridge
   C. At the opera
   D. Juniper Hills

Answers on page 351.

Track the Fugitive

The investigator is tracking the fugitive's past trips in order to find and recover information that was left behind in five cities. Each city was visited only once. Can you put together the travel timeline, using the information below?

1. The fugitive began in either Venice or Salerno.

2. The fugitive's final visit was to either Salerno or Turin.

3. The fugitive went to Bari before Genoa, but not immediately before.

4. The fugitive did not go from Genoa to Turin.

Answer on page 351.

Robber Riddle

Cryptograms are messages in substitution code. Break the code to read the message. For example, THE SMART CAT might become FVO QWGDF JGF if **F** is substituted for **T, V** for **H, O** for **E,** and so on.

AKZ FMF UKG OIDDGO UBNG B DBUK DGHIOG CIMSC

UI UKG DBSN?

DGWBXVG KG ABSUGF UI QBNG VXOG KG KBF B

WPGBS CGUBABZ.

Robber Riddle

Cryptograms are messages in substitution code. Break the code to read the message. For example, THE SMART CAT might become FVO QWGDF JGF if **F** is substituted for **T, V** for **H, O** for **E,** and so on.

DSB WRW GSV ILYYVI DVZI DSRGV TOLEVH?

SV WRWM'T DZMG GL YV XZFTSG IVW-SZMWVW.

Answers on pages 351/352.

DNA Sequence

Examine the two images below carefully. Are these sequences a match or not?

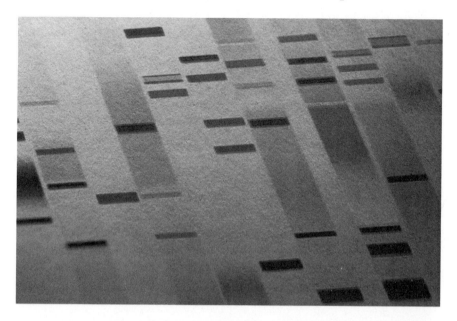

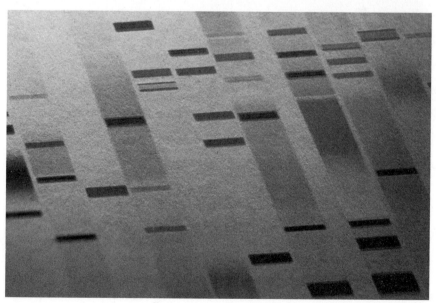

Answer on page 352.

Motel Hideout

A thief hides out in one of the 45 motel rooms listed in the chart below. The motel's in-house detective received a sheet of four clues, signed "The Logical Thief." Using these clues, the detective found the room number within 15 minutes—but by that time, the thief had fled. Can you find the thief's motel room more quickly?

1. The number is even.

2. The number is not divisible by 4 or 6.

3. The sum of the digits is a prime number.

4. Subtract 1 from the number. The result is not prime.

51	52	53	54	55	56	57	58	59
41	42	43	44	45	46	47	48	49
31	32	33	34	35	36	37	38	39
21	22	23	24	25	26	27	28	29
11	12	13	14	15	16	17	18	19

Answer on page 352.

Track the Fugitive

The investigator is tracking the fugitive's past trips in order to find and recover information that was left behind in five cities. Each city was visited only once. Can you put together the travel timeline, using the information below?

1. Manchester was the first, third, or fifth city visited.

2. The city in Wales was visited before the city in Scotland, but not immediately before.

3. Neither Sheffield nor Glasgow was the last city visited, but one of them was the fourth.

4. Swansea was visited immediately before Liverpool.

5. The visit to Sheffield did not immediately precede or follow a visit to Manchester, but it did follow a trip to another city in England.

The Serial Arsonist

A series of arson fires has plagued the sleepy little town of Villano Beach over the past several months. Five fires have been reported so far, each at a different location and each started at a different time. No two fires were set on the same day, and police are baffled by the fact that none of the five buildings seemed to share any similarities. Using only the clues below, determine the date, time and location of each fire, as well as the type of building each fire destroyed.

1. Of the two fires on First Avenue and Apple Street, one was started at 4:45 am and the other destroyed the surf shop.

2. The fire that started at 1:45 am was set sometime after the incident at the pizzeria.

3. The car wash fire was either the one set at 1:45 am or the one on March 3rd.

4. The book store fire was set at 3:10 am.

5. Of the fire at First Avenue and the one at the car wash, one was started at 4:45 am and the other was set on April 2nd.

6. The Twelfth Street fire, the one set on May 5th, the one started at 1:45 am, and the fire set on April 2nd were four separate incidents.

7. The Cranford Lane fire started at 1:45 am and was set sometime before June 15th.

8. The April 2nd fire didn't start at 1:15 am.

		Times					Locations					Buildings			
		1:15 am	1:45 am	2:30 am	3:10 am	4:45 am	Apple St.	Cranford Ln.	First Ave.	Nickel Dr.	Twelfth St.	bank	bookstore	car wash	pizzeria	surf shop
Dates	March 3															
	April 2															
	May 5															
	June 4															
	July 1															
Buildings	bank															
	bookstore															
	car wash															
	pizzeria															
	surf shop															
Locations	Apple St.															
	Cranford Ln.															
	First Ave.															
	Nickel Dr.															
	Twelfth St.															

Dates	Times	Locations	Buildings
March 3			
April 2			
May 5			
June 4			
July 1			

Track the Fugitive

The investigator is tracking the fugitive's past trips in order to find and recover information that was left behind in five cities. Each city was visited only once. Can you put together the travel timeline, using the information below?

1. Brasília, was one of the final two cities visited.

2. The trip to Caracas happened before the trip to Bogotá, but at least two other cities separated the visits.

3. From Valparaíso the fugitive went directly to either Bogotá or Brasília.

4. The fugitive did not begin her travels in Montevideo.

5. The fugitive did not travel directly from Chile to Brazil.

Answer on page 352.

In Plain Sight

Cryptograms are messages in substitution code. Break the code to read the message. For example, THE SMART CAT might become FVO QWGDF JGF if **F** is substituted for **T, V** for **H, O** for **E,** and so on.

LSIQ UVY KVQKIDA UVYB FICCDPI WQ DQVJSIB NVBF

VN JIMJ—NVB IMDFRAI, SWGWQP WQNVBFDJWVQ

WQ D PBVKIBU AWCJ VB D KADCCWNWIG DG—WJ WC

KDAAIG CJIPDQVPBDRSU. LBWJWQP D FICCDPI WQ

WQEWCWHAI WQX DQG LBWJWQP D BIPYADB FICCD-

PI VEIB WJ WC VQI NVBF VN CJIPDQVPBDRSU.

Jump on a Train

You're on a runaway train that won't stop moving forward! The path from start to finish must follow the curve of the loops; sharp turns aren't allowed.

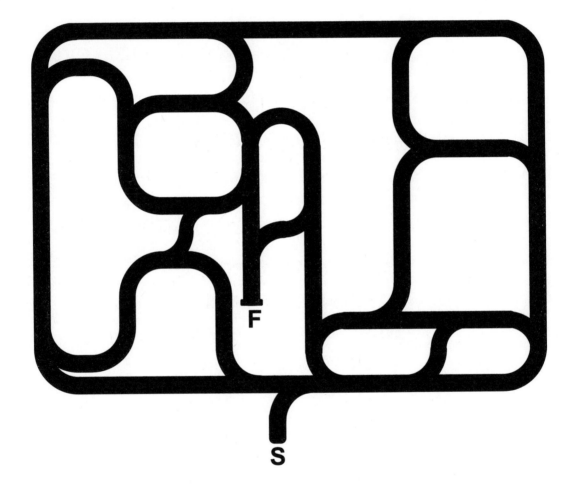

Answer on page 352.

Interception

You've intercepted a message that you think contains information about an upcoming meeting. The only problem is, it contains way too many possibilities! Can you figure out the details of the next meeting?

OCTOBER TEN

THE HEATH

ELEVATOR EIGHT

ESCALATOR DURING THE FULL MOON

TANZANIA IN MARCH

OVER AT THE GULF

JANUARY IN NASSAU

NOVEMBER AT THE CAFE

AT A NICE RESTAURANT

NEW MOON IN ORLANDO

OCTOBER AT NOON

ATLANTA IN A TENT

THURSDAY AT THE BEACH

EXPRESSWAY EXIT R

IN TEL-AVIV

EXACTLY MID-DECEMBER

BRIDGE IN VENEZUELA

NEVER AT THE SKATING RINK

Mystery Terminology

Every word listed is contained within the group of letters. Words can be found in a straight line horizontally, vertically, or diagonally. They may be read either forward or backward.

ANALYSIS	FINGERPRINT
CLUES	INTERVIEW
CONFESSION	JUSTICE
CRIMINAL	LARCENY
DOCUMENT	MOTIVE
EXAMINATION	PROOF
EYEWITNESS	SCENE
FACTS	THEFT

```
F I N T E R V I A C E C L U E S
M D N N S T C A F C Y G M W G E
J E E I T C A F D R E D I S C P
W C V F T E U O N I W D F R D R
S N H I U O C R I M I N A L D O
U T G S T U M T C I T L L A T O
F H O S M O F N O N N W N R A F
I E E E U S M I N I E E O C N L
N N N N S I D R F T G I I E I X
G T P T Y S O P E S E V S N M E
E N R I L Y C R S U A R S Y A C
R E O W A L U E S J L E E C X I
P C O E N A T G I N L T F C E T
R S G Y A N E N W O C N N L W S
C L U E X A M I N A T I O N D U
P D T F E H T F Y J I J C G G J
```

Track the Fugitive

The investigator is tracking the fugitive's past trips in order to find and recover information that was left behind in five cities. Each city was visited only once. Can you put together the travel timeline, using the information below?

1. The fugitive went from Brussels directly to the capital of Norway.

2. Osaka and the other city that started with O were neither the first nor last cities.

3. Barcelona was either the first or fourth city.

4. The trip to Munich was preceded immediately by a trip to Oslo.

Answer on page 353.

Seen at the Scene (Part I)

Study this picture of the crime scene for 1 minute, then turn the page.

Seen at the Scene (Part II)

(Do not read this until you have read the previous page!) Which image exactly matches the crime scene?

1.

2.

3.

4.

Answer on page 353.

Motel Hideout

A thief hides out in one of the 45 motel rooms listed in the chart below. The motel's in-house detective received a sheet of four clues, signed "The Logical Thief." Using these clues, the detective found the room number within 15 minutes—but by that time, the thief had fled. Can you find the thief's motel room more quickly?

1. The sum of the digits is less than 10.

2. When you multiply the digits together, the resulting number is less than 10.

3. The number is prime.

4. If you reverse the order of the digits, the resulting number is not found on the chart.

51	52	53	54	55	56	57	58	59
41	42	43	44	45	46	47	48	49
31	32	33	34	35	36	37	38	39
21	22	23	24	25	26	27	28	29
11	12	13	14	15	16	17	18	19

Answer on page 353.

Track the Fugitive

The investigator is tracking the fugitive's past trips in order to find and recover information that was left behind in five cities. Each city was visited only once. Can you put together the travel timeline, using the information below?

1. Cape Town was visited sometime before Casablanca.

2. Tripoli was visited sometime after Cairo, but not immediately after.

3. Kinshasa was one of the first three cities visited.

4. None of the cities that start with C were visited back to back.

Answer on page 353.

Race to a Solution

Cryptograms are messages in substitution code. Break the code to read the message. For example, THE SMART CAT might become FVO QWGDF JGF if **F** is substituted for **T, V** for **H, O** for **E,** and so on.

WDQGN WI GWNFX PWNGGN WO W CJPEGX, LBPE

DNWIPBO SGPWHG W HXOQGNX IJTGFBOQ. QYG HXO-

QGNBGO BI YBO KJKRFWN SGOQOGFFBIA IJTGFO JDQ-

GI YWL W PJIIGPQBJI QJ QYG SNBQBOY NWPBIA UJNFL.

Spotted at the _____ Store

The letters in ANTIQUE can be found in boxes 2, 6, 7, 8, 9, 10, and 14 but not necessarily in that order. Similarly, the letters in all the other types of stores can be found in the boxes indicated. Your task is to insert all the letters of the alphabet into the boxes. If you do this correctly, the shaded cells will reveal the name of another type of store.

Hint: Compare PET and PACKAGE to get the value of T, then PET and SHOE for the values of P and E.

Unused letters: X and Z

ANTIQUE: 2, 6, 7, 8, 9, 10, 14
BOOK: 5, 18, 19
CANDY: 1, 4, 7, 10, 12
CLOTHING: 2, 4, 5, 7, 8, 15, 16, 23
CONVENIENCE: 2, 4, 5, 7, 9, 22
DEPARTMENT: 1, 7, 8, 9, 10, 20, 21, 24
DRUG: 1, 6, 21, 23

FURNITURE: 2, 6, 7, 8, 9, 17, 21
GENERAL: 7, 9, 10, 15, 21, 23
GROCERY: 4, 5, 9, 12, 21, 23
HARDWARE: 1, 9, 10, 13, 16, 21
JEWELRY: 9, 11, 12, 13, 15, 21
PACKAGE: 4, 9, 10, 19, 20, 23
PET: 8, 9, 20
SHOE: 3, 5, 9, 16

1	2	3	4	5	6	7	8	9	10	11	12	13

14	15	16	17	18	19	20	21	22	23	24	25	26
											X	Z

60

Answers on page 353.

Overheard Information (Part I)

Read the story below, then turn the page and answer the questions.

A postal worker overheard a conversation between two men who were speaking in hushed tones on the corner of First Street and Victoria Avenue this morning: "Mr. White has given us three targets for Saturday's bomb threats. All three are to be detonated at precisely 1:45pm unless our demands have been met. First is the electrical substation on Wallace Drive. Second, the Bell River Dam up by Bayside. And third, Wilson's Savings and Loan on the corner of Paulsen Drive and Tether Lane. Once all three bombs are placed we will call in our demands - $10 million in unmarked $100 bills to be left under a park bench in Beaumont Park. Sandy will make pick up the cash if all goes to plan."

Overheard Information (Part II)

(Do not read this until you have read the previous page!)

1. **How many sites will have bombs placed at them?**
   A. two
   B. three
   C. four
   D. five

2. **Which of the following is NOT going to be a target?**
   A. sheriff's office
   B. savings and loan
   C. electrical substation
   D. dam

3. **On what corner were the two suspicious men having their conversation?**
   A. Paulsen and Tether
   B. Bayside and Wallace
   C. Clark and Valencia
   D. First and Victoria

4. **Where will the $10 million in unmarked bills be dropped?**
   A. Beaumont Park
   B. Bayside Park
   C. Bell River Park
   D. Bertram Park

Answers on page 354.

A Lady of Mystery

Cryptograms are messages in substitution code. Break the code to read the message. For example, THE SMART CAT might become FVO QWGDF JGF if **F** is substituted for **T, V** for **H, O** for **E,** and so on.

Z.P. JDRTF, HWCU ZEVOOGF PWCWIEV JDRTF, QDF D

HCGIGFE LCGRT QCGITC. ETC ZCWIDBWUGFI QDF

ZWOGLT LWRRDUPTC DPDR PDOBOGTFE, QEW DOFW

QCWIT ZWTICV. FET QDF BGNTU IET IGIOT WX HD-

CWUTFF ODITC GU OGXT.

DNA Sequence

Examine the two images below carefully. Are these sequences a match or not?

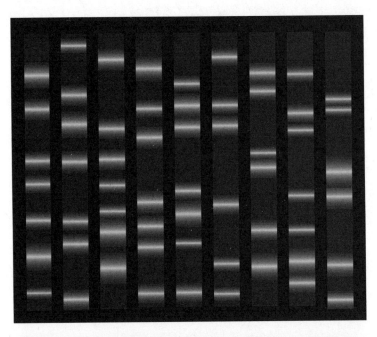

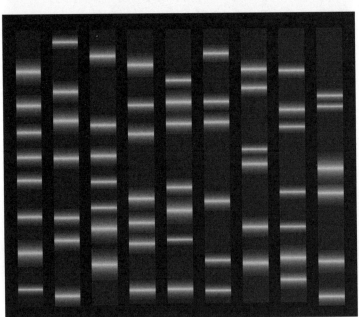

Answer on page 354.

Robber Riddle

Cryptograms are messages in substitution code. Break the code to read the message. For example, THE SMART CAT might become FVO QWGDF JGF if **F** is substituted for **T, V** for **H, O** for **E,** and so on.

BWD NXN IWO LJGVQKG TUOS WXH HKMZ BWOS XI

HIKGION IT GKXS?

WO BKH WTUXSV PTG HTRO MWKSVO XS IWO BOKI-

WOG.

Robber Riddle

Cryptograms are messages in substitution code. Break the code to read the message. For example, THE SMART CAT might become FVO QWGDF JGF if **F** is substituted for **T, V** for **H, O** for **E,** and so on.

SDU SWO PDA PDEAB WHH SAP?

DA PNEAZ PK NKX A NERANXWJG.

Motel Hideout

A thief hides out in one of the 45 motel rooms listed in the chart below. The motel's in-house detective received a sheet of four clues, signed "The Logical Thief." Using these clues, the detective found the room number within 15 minutes—but by that time, the thief had fled. Can you find the thief's motel room more quickly?

1. The number is prime.

2. The second digit is larger than the first.

3. If you multiply the digits, the resulting number is prime.

4. The sum of the digits is less than 7.

51	52	53	54	55	56	57	58	59
41	42	43	44	45	46	47	48	49
31	32	33	34	35	36	37	38	39
21	22	23	24	25	26	27	28	29
11	12	13	14	15	16	17	18	19

Answer on page 354.

Pick Your Poison

There are four bottles before you, but they've gotten jumbled up. Poison is found in one of them. If you arrange them from left to right, following the instructions given below, you will be able to know where the poison is found.

1. Two bottles are red, and they are not next to each other.

2. The pink bottle is either the second bottle from the left or the bottle at the far right.

3. The poison is in the bottle between the two bottles of the same color.

4. The pink bottle is not next to the bottle with the poison nor does it contain the poison.

5. The orange bottle is not next to the pink bottle.

Baddies of Fiction

ACROSS

1. Hot rocks
5. Boggy land
8. Belch, say
12. "Deliver us from ___"
13. "Do the Right Thing" director
14. Hip-hop trio Salt-N-___
15. Count calories
16. Archer's wood
17. Arrogant sort
18. "The Demon Barber of Fleet Street"
21. 1985 Kurosawa classic
22. A in German class?
23. Coal worker
26. "The Big Bang Theory" character from India
27. Barrel at a bash
30. "Nightmare on Elm Street" villain
33. It's often left hanging
34. A pal of Pooh
35. Easy gait
36. Big embrace
37. "Fifth Beatle" Yoko
38. "Psycho" weirdo
43. Sonny or Chastity
44. "___ culpa"
45. "Don't worry about me"
47. Orders a dog to attack
48. Escort's offering
49. 1980s Dodge model
50. "Iliad" war god
51. "___ Skylark" (Shelley)
52. Apollo acronym

DOWN

1. Blazed a trail
2. Alamo alternative
3. Panoramic sight
4. Did a tailoring job
5. Robin Hood portrayer Errol
6. Bigfoot's shoe size?
7. It begins in January
8. Big name in printers
9. Fix, as socks
10. It can help you carry a tune
11. Eatery check
19. Body part that vibrates

20. Baja border city
23. Artist's degree
24. Abbr. on a clothing reject tag
25. Hoop hanger
26. "King Kong" and "Citizen Kane" studio
27. C.I.A.'s Soviet counterpart
28. Aquarium wriggler
29. College sr.'s exam
31. Something to meditate on
32. Feeling

36. 1990s candidate ___ Perot
37. 2009 Peace Prize Nobelist
38. "Film ___" (dark movie genre)
39. "The Raven" start
40. "Fiddling" emperor
41. Madame Bovary
42. Heirs, often
43. "Be prepared" org.
46. Cadenza maker

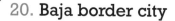

Which Sleuth Was He Again?

Cryptograms are messages in substitution code. Break the code to read the message. For example, THE SMART CAT might become FVO QWGDF JGF if **F** is substituted for **T, V** for **H, O** for **E,** and so on.

HNVCHGYW IBDEGK CSEWYU KHY CEGK BA IBKH JEV

JCEUY, IEJYU BZ UEJHLYSS HEVVYKK'J ALOKLBZES UY-

KYOKLQY LZ "KHY VESKYJY AESOBZ," EZU CHLSLC

VEGSBRY, CGBKEDBZLJK BA GEWVBZU OHEZUSYG'J

"KHY ILD JSYYC."

Answer on page 355.

Motel Hideout

A thief hides out in one of the 45 motel rooms listed in the chart below. The motel's in-house detective received a sheet of four clues, signed "The Logical Thief." Using these clues, the detective found the room number within 15 minutes—but by that time, the thief had fled. Can you find the thief's motel room more quickly?

1. The number is divisible by 3.

2. The first digit and the second digit are not consecutive numbers (for example, neither 12 nor 54).

3. The number is not divisible by 11, 13, 15, 17, or 19.

4. If you multiply the digits together, the result is neither a multiple of 8 nor contains the digit 8.

51	52	53	54	55	56	57	58	59
41	42	43	44	45	46	47	48	49
31	32	33	34	35	36	37	38	39
21	22	23	24	25	26	27	28	29
11	12	13	14	15	16	17	18	19

Answer on page 355.

Law Enforcement Equipment

Every word listed is contained within the group of letters. Words can be found in a straight line horizontally, vertically, or diagonally. They may be read either forward or backward.

BADGES	HOLSTERS
BALLISTIC VEST	PEPPER SPRAY
BATONS	RADIOS
BODY ARMOR	RESTRAINTS
CAMERAS	RIOT GEAR
DUTY BELT	SHIELDS
EYEWEAR	STUN GUN
FLASHLIGHTS	TACTICAL BAGS
HELMET	UNIFORMS

```
G I L H S A L F R S G N U T S S
P T U N I F O R W A N G R S D H
E S S T U N G U N P E O E U L I
P E P P E R S P R A Y G T V R E
P V R F S E Y E W E D Y T A W L
E C E W R O T A B A B E R O B D
R I M L E L H S B E S S E T I S
S T A C T I C A L B A G S L N R
P S C U S O I D A R B V T E I T
O I B A L L I S T I C V R B A H
G L U U O M R A Y D O B A Y R O
F L A S H L I G H T S R I T T L
R A D I N M S M R O F I N U S S
U B O D Y A R M O R V N T D E T
H E L M H E L M E T S I S U R E
R A E W E Y E V V S A R E M A C
```

The Check Bouncer

Detective Amanda Berenson is investigating a series of five bad checks that have bounced around the neighborhood of Jessup Hill. So far five bad checks have been reported, and she suspects, based on handwriting analysis, that one person is behind all five incidents (each of which happened at a different location and involved a check with a different fake name). Using only the clues below, match each bounced check to its date, name and amount, and determine the location at which each was used.

1. The check passed on Wallace Way was worth $75 more than the one signed by "Roger Rose."

2. Of the "Ted Mobius" check and the one used on July 13th, one was passed at a deli on Ball Boulevard and the other was for $550.

3. The check signed by "Roger Rose" (which was dated July 30th) was either the one for $400 or the one used at an electronics store on Smith Street.

4. The $325 check is either the one signed by "Ned Steel" or the one used at the Ball Boulevard deli.

5. The amount on the July 30th check was $75 less than the amount on the check dated August 12th.

6. The check used on Ball Boulevard was worth $75 less than the one dated August 15th.

7. "Ted Mobius" signed the check for $400.

8. The $475 check wasn't used on Raptor Road, and the most expensive check wasn't signed by "Owen Pierce."

	Dates					Locations					Fake Names				
	July 13th	July 30th	August 4th	August 12th	August 15th	Ball Blvd.	Lincoln Ln.	Raptor Rd.	Smith St.	Wallace Way	Ned Steel	Owen Pierce	Pedro Hope	Roger Rose	Ted Mobius
Amounts $250															
$325															
$400															
$475															
$550															
Fake Names Ned Steel															
Owen Pierce															
Pedro Hope															
Roger Rose															
Ted Mobius															
Locations Ball Blvd.															
Lincoln Ln.															
Raptor Rd.															
Smith St.															
Wallace Way															

Amounts	Dates	Locations	Fake Names
$250			
$325			
$400			
$475			
$550			

Aristocratic Accomplices

The letters in BARONESS can be found in boxes 1, 2, 3, 4, 5, 8, and 19 but not necessarily in that order. Similarly, the letters in all the other titled ladies can be found in the boxes indicated. Your task is to insert all the letters of the alphabet into the boxes. If you do this correctly, the shaded cells will reveal the name of other titled ladies.

Hint: Compare MISS and MILADY to get the value of S, then MISS and RANI for the values of M and I.

Unused letters: J, K, and X

BARONESS: 1, 2, 3, 4, 5, 8, 19

CROWN PRINCESS: 1, 2, 3, 4, 5, 6, 12, 15, 23

CZARINA: 3, 5, 6, 8, 9, 23

DAME: 2, 8, 10, 18

FRAU: 5, 8, 16, 20

GRAND DUCHESS: 1, 2, 3, 5, 8, 10, 11, 16, 22, 23

MADAME: 2, 8, 10, 18

MADEMOISELLE: 1, 2, 4, 6, 8, 10, 17, 18

MAHARANI: 3, 5, 6, 8, 11, 18

MILADY: 6, 8, 10, 14, 17, 18

MISS: 1, 6, 18

QUEEN: 2, 3, 13, 16

RANI: 3, 5, 6, 8

SENORA: 1, 2, 3, 4, 5, 8

VICECOUNTESS: 1, 2, 3, 4, 6, 7, 16, 21, 23

1	2	3	4	5	6	7	8	9	10	11	12	13
14	15	16	17	18	19	20	21	22	23	24	25	26
										J	K	X

Answers on page 355.

Methods of Disguise

Unscramble each word or phrase below to reveal a word or phrase related to disguises.

EACH MUST

HAYRIDE (2 words)

CAPABLE LABS (2 words)

HA RICE FAIL (2 words)

SAG LESS

AN AND BAN

LA LAVA CAB

DEBAR

UM PEAK

SUN BRIDES

RUM LABEL

PRO ALAS

Answers on page 355.

Pick Your Poison

There are four bottles before you, but they've gotten jumbled up. Poison is found in one of them. If you arrange them from left to right, following the instructions given below, you will be able to know where the poison is found.

1. The blue bottle is to the right of the purple bottle, but not immediately to the right.

2. The yellow bottle is not next to the purple bottle.

3. The brown bottle and the white bottle are next to each other.

4. The white bottle is next to the yellow bottle.

5. The poison is found in the bottle that is the second from the left.

Answer on page 355.

Read the story below, then turn the page and answer the questions.

A woman who lives near Bradleyburg Prison overheard two men having a particularly suspicious conversation this morning. One was pointing to the southwest fence corner and said: "That's the spot. 2:00 am Wednesday, our guard on the inside, Milton, will shut down all cameras and motion detectors in the southwest quadrant before opening up cells B-15, B-21 and C-5. The two guys in each of those cells will have eight minutes to reach that section of fence in between room checks. Stacy will be there with bolt cutters to cut out a large enough hole for them to fit through, and Jolene will have the getaway van ready just two blocks away. We all regroup Thursday night, 6:00 pm, at the safe house in Burlington."

Overheard Information
(Part II)

(Do not read this until you have read the previous page!)

1. How many prisoners will take part in this escape?

   A. four
   B. three
   C. six
   D. eight

2. How much time passes between each nightly room check?

   A. fifteen minutes
   B. thirty minutes
   C. eight minutes
   D. one hour

3. Who is driving the getaway van?

   A. Stacey
   B. Jolene
   C. Bradley
   D. Milton

4. Which part of the prison fence will be used in the escape?

   A. northwest corner
   B. southeast corner
   C. southwest corner
   D. northeast corner

Answers on page 355.

Flee the Scene

Navigate the twisting path to track down the person of interest.

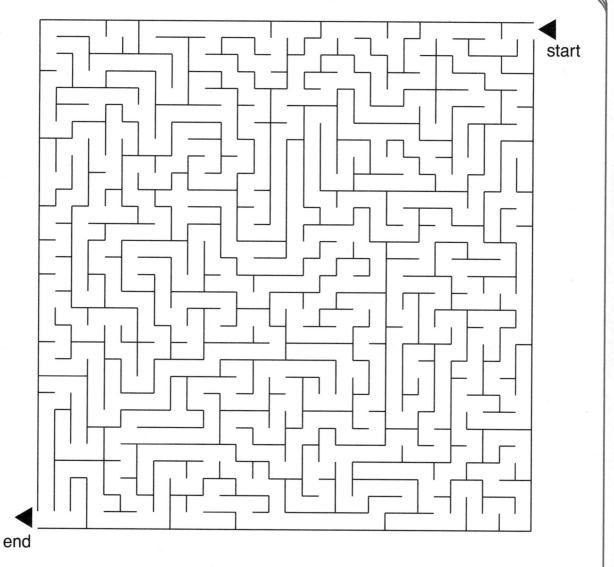

start

end

Answer on page 356.

A Mystery from History

Cryptograms are messages in substitution code. Break the code to read the message. For example, THE SMART CAT might become FVO QWGDF JGF if **F** is substituted for **T, V** for **H, O** for **E,** and so on.

GSP ITQMWOS NKMHFOCWXG WF K RKNTHF NKMH-

FOCWXG GSKG SKF OSKDDPMUPV OCQXGTUCKXSP-

CF. GSP NKMHFOCWXG FHXXTFPVDQ VKGPF BKOE GT

GSP PKCDQ RWRGPPMGS OPMGHCQ. WG OTMGKWMF

VCKJWMUF TR XDKMGF KMV TGSPC TBZPOGF KOOT-

NXKMWPV BQ GPLG, BHG MT TMP SKF BPPM KBDP GT

VPOWXSPC GSP GPLG.

Answer on page 356.

Track the Fugitive

The investigator is tracking the fugitive's past trips in order to find and recover information that was left behind in five cities. Each city was visited only once. Can you put together the travel timeline, using the information below?

1. The fugitive did not travel from Houston to San Antonio or vice versa.

2. The fugitive traveled to Louisville from Eugene, with a stop at one other city in between.

3. The fugitive traveled from one city that starts with "San" immediately to the next, in alphabetical order.

4. Houston was not the last city visited.

5. San Diego was one of the first three cities visited.

Answer on page 356.

Interception

You've intercepted two messages between criminal masterminds. One informed you they would be meeting in a European city on a specific date. The other is the list of European cities seen below. The only problem is, the message shows many European cities, not just one. Can you figure out the right location?

PRAGUE

TALLINN

WARSAW

SOFIA

BRUSSELS

Answer on page 356.

Seen at the Scene (Part I)

Study this picture of the crime scene for 1 minute, then turn the page.

Seen at the Scene (Part II)

(Do not read this until you have read the previous page!)

Which image exactly matches the picture from the previous page?

1.

2.

3.

4.

Answer on page 356.

Overhead Information (Part I)

Read the story below, then turn the page and answer the questions.

A janitor at Ford Hill University overheard a conversation between two students who seemed to be angry about their recent football loss to Ridgedale College: "We'll get them back, don't you worry... Casey, Tom and Linda will show up at Ridgedale's East Campus on the night of the 16th. Linda is a master lock-picker, she'll be able to get them into the arena's mascot room in no time. Once Casey and Tom have stolen their mascot, Pepper the Pig, they'll bundle him into their Toyota 4Runner and hightail it down to Casey's uncle's cabin up in Montvale. The pig is still pretty small – he only weighs about 40 pounds – so he should fit in there, no problem. The plan is to lay low for four days before they will leave Pepper tied to a tree in Grant Park on the 20th... wearing a Ford Hill scarf of gold and blue, naturally! We'll be the talk of the campus after this!"

Overhead Information (Part II)

(Do not read this until you have read the previous page!)

1. Who is the master lock-picker of the group?
   A. Casey
   B. Tom
   C. Dale
   D. Linda

2. What is the mascot pig's name?
   A. Pepper
   B. Penny
   C. Parsley
   D. Pauline

3. How many days do they intend to hold on to the pig?
   A. two
   B. seven
   C. five
   D. four

4. What gold-and-blue item will the pig be wearing when it is finally left to be discovered in Grant Park?
   A. scarf
   B. hat
   C. t-shirt
   D. socks

Answers on page 356.

Motel Hideout

A thief hides out in one of the 45 motel rooms listed in the chart below. The motel's in-house detective received a sheet of four clues, signed "The Logical Thief." Using these clues, the detective found the room number within 10 minutes—but by that time, the thief had fled. Can you find the thief's motel room more quickly?

1. 3 is one of the digits.

2. The number is not prime.

3. The sum of the digits is larger than 5.

4. The number is divisible by 4.

51	52	53	54	55	56	57	58	59
41	42	43	44	45	46	47	48	49
31	32	33	34	35	36	37	38	39
21	22	23	24	25	26	27	28	29
11	12	13	14	15	16	17	18	19

Answer on page 356.

More Mystery Terminology

Every word listed is contained within the group of letters. Words can be found in a straight line horizontally, vertically, or diagonally. They may be read either forward or backward.

ACCIDENT REPORT	INVESTIGATION
ACCOMPLICE	JAILCELL
ALIBI	MIRANDA RIGHTS
BAIL	POLICE
COURTROOM	POLYGRAPH
DETAIN	PROBABLE CAUSE
DETECTIVE	SENTENCE
EVIDENCE	SURVEILLANCE
HANDCUFFS	WARRANT

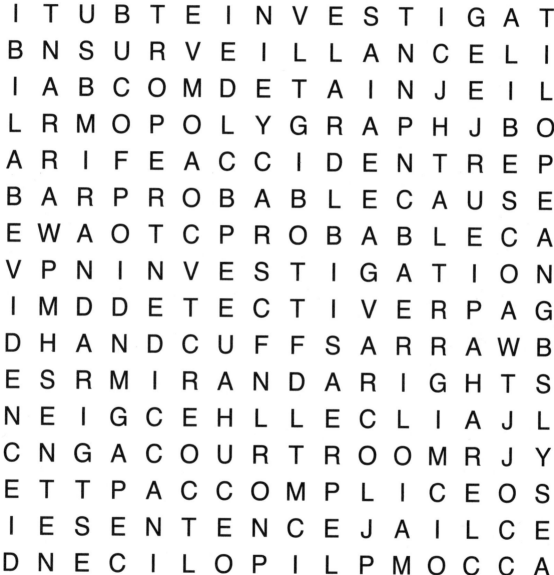

```
I T U B T E I N V E S T I G A T
B N S U R V E I L L A N C E L I
I A B C O M D E T A I N J E I L
L R M O P O L Y G R A P H J B O
A R I F E A C C I D E N T R E P
B A R P R O B A B L E C A U S E
E W A O T C P R O B A B L E C A
V P N I N V E S T I G A T I O N
I M D D E T E C T I V E R P A G
D H A N D C U F F S A R R A W B
E S R M I R A N D A R I G H T S
N E I G C E H L L E C L I A J L
C N G A C O U R T R O O M R J Y
E T T P A C C O M P L I C E O S
I E S E N T E N C E J A I L C E
D N E C I L O P I L P M O C C A
```

The Graffiti Gang

The town of Cordilla Hills has a serious graffiti problem. A gang of five graffiti artists has been spray painting their tags all over town. Law enforcement knows their individual names but they still need help to build a case against the gang. Help them out by matching each graffiti artist to his or her unique neighborhood, the two colors of paint they use (no two members use the same two colors) and the total number of graffiti tags each has painted.

1. Neither Daryl nor the graffiti artist who uses cyan and silver paint works Downtown.

2. Of Lucretia and the suspect who works on the East Side, one has 29 known tags and the other uses only orange and teal spray paint.

3. The person who uses cyan and silver paint (who isn't Clarence) has 14 more tags than whoever works Uptown, and 14 fewer tags than Agatha.

4. Lucretia has 7 fewer tags than the person who works exclusively with gray and purple spray paint.

5. The five suspects are Daryl, Lucretia, the person with 36 tags, the one who works in Midtown, and the one who uses cyan and silver paint.

6. The tags found in Midtown don't use green or white paint.

		Name					Neighborhood					Colors				
		Agatha	Clarence	Daryl	Lucretia	Patrick	Downtown	East Side	Midtown	Uptown	West Side	blue & pink	cyan & silver	gray & purple	green & white	orange & teal
Tags	15															
	22															
	29															
	36															
	43															
Colors	blue & pink															
	cyan & silver															
	gray & purple															
	green & white															
	orange & teal															
Neighborhood	Downtown															
	East Side															
	Midtown															
	Uptown															
	West Side															

Tags	Name	Neighborhood	Colors
15			
22			
29			
36			
43			

Track the Fugitive

The investigator is tracking the fugitive's past trips in order to find and recover information that was left behind in five cities. Each city was visited only once. Can you put together the travel timeline, using the information below?

1. The fugitive went from Denver directly to New Orleans.

2. The fugitive did not go from New Orleans to either Indianapolis or Portland.

3. Hartford was not the last city on the fugitive's list.

4. The fugitive went to Indianapolis before Portland, but not immediately before.

Answer on page 357.

DNA Sequence

Examine the two images below carefully. Are these sequences a match or not?

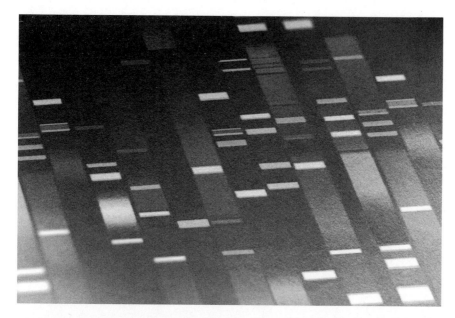

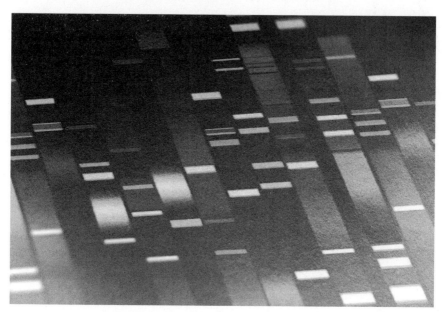

Motel Hideout

A thief hides out in one of the 45 motel rooms listed in the chart below. The motel's in-house detective received a sheet of four clues, signed "The Logical Thief." Using these clues, the detective found the room number within 15 minutes—but by that time, the thief had fled. Can you find the thief's motel room more quickly?

1. The number is not divisible by 4.

2. The first digit is as large or larger than the second digit.

3. The digits add up to 6.

4. The number is divisible by 6.

51	52	53	54	55	56	57	58	59
41	42	43	44	45	46	47	48	49
31	32	33	34	35	36	37	38	39
21	22	23	24	25	26	27	28	29
11	12	13	14	15	16	17	18	19

Answer on page 357.

Bank Robbery Alert
(Part I)

A community bank was robbed this week in Winterdale. The following information has been gleaned from eyewitness statements. Read it carefully before turning the page to see how many details you can remember.

Date: Wednesday, April 13, 2021

Time: 3:10 to 3:18pm

Suspect descriptions:

Suspect #1: Fair-skinned female, 5'2", short red hair, wearing sunglasses and a white face mask. Tattoo of a snake on left forearm. Referred to as "Ginger" by the second suspect. Brandished a small handgun.

Suspect #2: Medium-complexion male, 6'4" with a goatee and shoulder-length black hair. Wore sunglasses and a green face mask. Witnesses saw a gold ring with a large blue inset stone on the fourth finger of his right hand. Name not mentioned. Brandished a machine gun with a wood-grain handle.

Getaway vehicle: Suspects left the scene in a silver convertible with Maryland license plates ending in M98, male suspect drove.

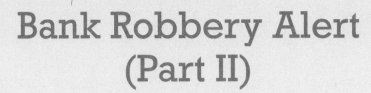

Bank Robbery Alert
(Part II)

(Do not read this until you have read the previous page!)

1. Which of the two suspects had a tattoo?

   _____

2. Describe the two weapons used during the robbery.

   _____

3. Which suspect was wearing a ring, and what color was the stone?

   _____

4. On what day of the week did the robbery occur?

   _____

Answers on page 357.

Adding Insult to Injury

Cryptograms are messages in substitution code. Break the code to read the message. For example, THE SMART CAT might become FVO QWGDF JGF if **F** is substituted for **T, V** for **H, O** for **E,** and so on.

1994 RVW SBF SBFAS LA V UFPRCLI LA FKUVPK HTINB'R

MVCISCIJ "SBF RNPFVH" APLH V JVGGFPY CI LRGL. SBF

SBCFUFR GFAS QFBCIK V ILSF SBVIECIJ SBF HTRFTH

ALP MLLP RFNTPCSY. SBF GVRS GVTJB WVR LI SBF

HTRFTH, SBLTJB, VR MLGCNF PFNLUFPFK SBF MVCISCIJ

VIK NVTJBS SBF SBCFUFR.

Over, Under, and Out

Cross over and under bridges to reach the end of this maze.

Enter

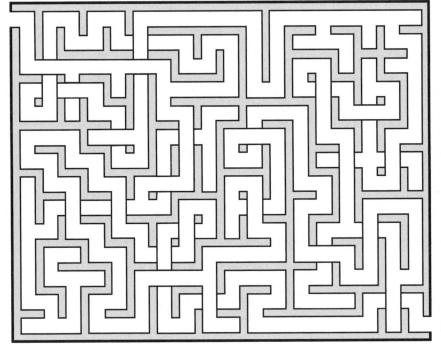

Exit

Answer on page 357.

To the Point

Unscramble each word or phrase below to reveal an object that might be used for murder.

HER BALD

PARSE

EVIL JAN

ALE ROMP

ROAN HOP

VIE GAL

TAN AGAIN

LEA EXPO

Track the Fugitive

The investigator is tracking the fugitive's past trips in order to find and recover information that was left behind in five cities. Each city was visited only once. Can you put together the travel timeline, using the information below?

1. From Philadelphia, the fugitive went to a Midwestern city.

2. The fugitive did not go to Charleston last.

3. The fugitive's first spot was either Omaha or San Jose.

4. The fugitive went to Boston sometime before Philadelphia.

5. At least one city separated the trip from San Jose and the trip to Charleston.

Answer on page 358.

Motel Hideout

A thief hides out in one of the 45 motel rooms listed in the chart below. The motel's in-house detective received a sheet of four clues, signed "The Logical Thief." Using these clues, the detective found the room number within 15 minutes—but by that time, the thief had fled. Can you find the thief's motel room more quickly?

1. The number is even.

2. The second digit is larger than the first.

3. The number is divisible by 4.

4. The number is not divisible by 6 or 7.

51	52	53	54	55	56	57	58	59
41	42	43	44	45	46	47	48	49
31	32	33	34	35	36	37	38	39
21	22	23	24	25	26	27	28	29
11	12	13	14	15	16	17	18	19

Answer on page 358.

DNA Sequence

Examine the two images below carefully. Are these sequences a match or not?

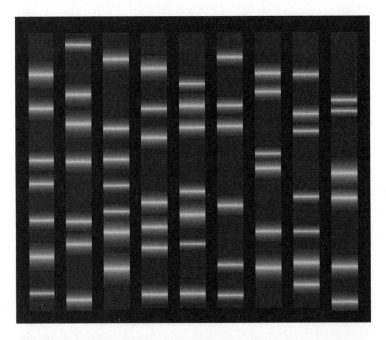

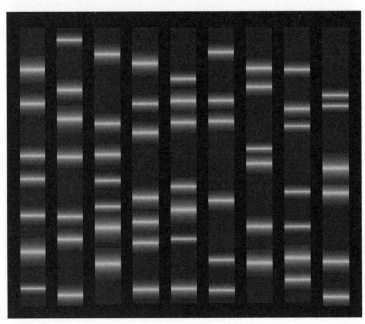

Answer on page 358.

AKA: Partner in Crime

The letters in ANGEL can be found in boxes 1, 4, 8, 9, and 21 but not necessarily in that order. Similarly, the letters in all the other terms of endearment listed below can be found in the boxes indicated. Your task is to insert all the letters of the alphabet into the boxes. If you do this correctly, the shaded cells will reveal another loving nickname.

Hint: Compare SWEETIE and SWEETHEART to get the value of I, then DEAR to DARLING for the value of E.

Unused letters: J, Q, and Z

ANGEL: 1, 4, 8, 9, 21
BABYDOLL: 1, 2, 8, 11, 15, 18
BUTTERCUP: 4, 5, 10, 13, 14, 18, 22
DARLING: 1, 5, 8, 9, 11, 20, 21
DEAR: 4, 5, 8, 11
DUMPLING: 1, 9, 11, 12, 14, 20, 21, 22
FOXY LADY: 1, 2, 6, 8, 11, 15, 19
HONEYBUNCH: 2, 4, 10, 14, 15, 17, 18, 21
LAMBKIN: 1, 8, 12, 16, 18, 20, 21
LOVE OF MY LIFE: 1, 2, 3, 4, 12, 15, 19, 20
SNOOKUMS: 2, 7, 12, 14, 16, 21
SUGAR: 5, 7, 8, 9, 14
SWEETHEART: 4, 5, 7, 8, 13, 17, 23
SWEETIE: 4, 7, 13, 20, 23
TREASURE: 4, 5, 7, 8, 13, 14

1		14	
2		15	
3		16	
4		17	
5		18	
6		19	
7		20	
8		21	
9		22	
10		23	
11		24	J
12		25	Q
13		26	Z

Police Lineups

Every word listed is contained within the group of letters. Words can be found in a straight line horizontally, vertically, or diagonally. They may be read either forward or backward.

ANONYMITY

BIAS

CONFIDENCE RATING

CULPRIT

FACING

FILLERS

IDENTITY PARADE

LOADING

ONE-WAY MIRROR

PHOTO ARRAY

PROFILE

PUTATIVE ID

SHOW-UP

SUSPECT

VICTIM

WITNESS

```
T I R P L U C I M Y N O N A C P
C G T R O R R I M Y A W E N O R
I A E P S U S W B I A S P N N O
V R R I U S U S P E C T L G F F
S E D A R A P Y T I T N E D I I
R C R P L N U T E L L I F H D L
E N A P H O T O A R R A Y P E F
L E P R T N A B C U L P R S N G
L D Y I S Y T D H S F M T P C N
I I S M H M I W I A S P A U E I
F F I Y O I V D C N R E W T R C
B N P A W T E I A O G I N A A A
I O N W U Y I L F O T C A T T F
A C E E P U D I S N L D G I I M
F B D N T A L E E S H O W V N W
E I I O C E V M I T C I V E G H
```

A Vendor of Death

Cryptograms are messages in substitution code. Break the code to read the message. For example, THE SMART CAT might become FVO QWGDF JGF if **F** is substituted for **T, V** for **H, O** for **E,** and so on.

AQXEAXG LIAOIGPN BRAEAX QIVXGX EASPK AG QJP

1600O. OJP KPSPEILPK X LIAOIG YXEEPK XMRX QIVX-

GX XGK OIEK AQ QI TIFPG EIIDAGB QI FRNKPN QJPAN

JROHXGKO. TJPG QJP LIEAYP YXFP VIN JPN, OJP VEPK

XGK OIRBJQ OXGYQRXNW AG X YJRNYJ; EIYXEO BNX-

QPVRE VIN JPN LNPSAIRO JPEL LNIQPYQPK JPN. PSPGQ-

RXEEW, JITPSPN, OJP TXO XNNPOQPK XGK PUPYRQPK,

XEIGB TAQJ JPN KXRBJQPN XGK OPSPNXE IQJPN XY-

YIFLEAYPO.

Answer on page 358.

Track the Fugitive

The investigator is tracking the fugitive's past trips in order to find and recover information that was left behind in five cities. Each city was visited only once. Can you put together the travel timeline, using the information below?

1. Vancouver was not the final city visited.

2. Toledo was not the first city.

3. At least one other stop separated the visit to Seattle and the later visit to San Diego.

4. Either Seattle or Richmond was the second city visited.

5. Vancouver was visited before Seattle.

6. Richmond was visited immediately before Toledo.

Fingerprint Match

Which fingerprint matches the one in the box?

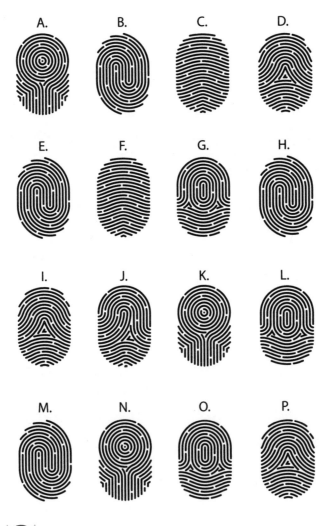

A.   B.   C.   D.

E.   F.   G.   H.

I.   J.   K.   L.

M.   N.   O.   P.

Answer on page 359.

Bank Robbery Alert
(Part I)

First Credit Bank was robbed this morning! The following information has been gleaned from eyewitness statements. Read it carefully before turning the page to see how many details you can remember.

Date: Thursday, June 3, 2021

Time: 10:32 to 10:49 am

Suspect descriptions: Three white males, each wearing masks

Suspect #1: 5'3", fair complexion, spoke with a heavy New Jersey accent. Brandished a Smith & Wesson 642 but never used it. Referred to as "Billy Boy" by the other two men.

Suspect #2: 5'11", with badly sunburned skin, wore eyeglasses and had a long blonde ponytail. Shot his Glock 43 twice into the ceiling upon entering the building. Never spoke.

Suspect #3: 6'8", darker complexion, spoke softly with an Eastern European accent. Was the only man to physically enter the bank vault, and he came out carrying two large bags of money. Not seen carrying any weapon.

Getaway vehicle: Suspects left the scene in a large Mercedes van with Florida license plates ending in 663. The shortest suspect was in the driver's seat.

Bank Robbery Alert (Part II)

(Do not read this until you have read the previous page!)

1. Describe the shortest of the three men with as much detail as possible.

   _____

2. How many shots were fired during the robbery?

   _____

3. Describe with as much detail as possible the man with sunburned skin.

   _____

   _____

4. How much time elapsed from the beginning of the robbery until the end?

   _____

Answers on page 359.

Crime Rhymes

Each clue leads to a 2-word answer that rhymes, such as BIG PIG or STABLE TABLE. The numbers in parentheses after the clue give the number of letters in each word. For example, "cookware taken from the oven (3, 3)" would be "hot pot."

1. Murder amongst Neanderthals (10, 7): _____

2. Person who wants to be a PI (11, 9): _____

3. When the police officer likes to play hockey in spare time (6, 12): _____

4. An investigator who specializes in crimes involving dental work (5, 6): _____

5. A line of people waiting at the detective's door (7, 5): _____

6. The detective called the fingerprint found on the candy cane this (10, 5): _____

7. The local ornithological society was horrified when a member was killed in what was later called this (6, 6): _____

8. The case of the poison being found in the toothpaste was called this (8, 8): _____

Interception

You've intercepted a message. You think it might be the location of a meeting between two criminals, but it doesn't seem to make sense. Can you decipher the true message?

CELERY TOO TWO OAT AGAIN GAZING EARTHWARDS

FIXING RIVER ZOO VEER VANE

IS SOON NEW

NEAR OVAL BOO MOVE

WANE ILL RIG HAT PAT

Answer on page 359.

Seen at the Scene (Part I)

Study this picture of the crime scene for 1 minute, then turn the page.

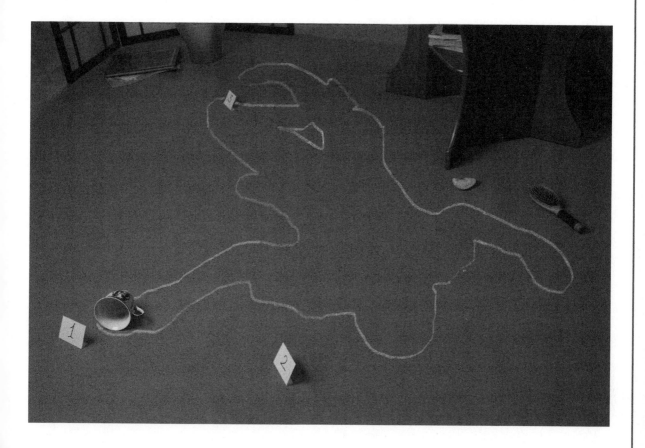

Seen at the Scene (Part II)

(Do not read this until you have read the previous page!) Which image exactly matches the crime scene?

1.

2.

3.

4.

Answer on page 359.

Motel Hideout

A thief hides out in one of the 45 motel rooms listed in the chart below. The motel's in-house detective received a sheet of four clues, signed "The Logical Thief." Using these clues, the detective found the room number within 15 minutes—but by that time, the thief had fled. Can you find the thief's motel room more quickly?

1. The number is either a multiple of 4 or has 4 as one of its digits, but not both.

2. The number is not divisible by 6, 7, or 8.

3. The first digit is larger than the second digit.

4. The number is not prime.

51	52	53	54	55	56	57	58	59
41	42	43	44	45	46	47	48	49
31	32	33	34	35	36	37	38	39
21	22	23	24	25	26	27	28	29
11	12	13	14	15	16	17	18	19

Answer on page 359.

Criminal Synonyms

Every word listed is contained within the group of letters. Words can be found in a straight line horizontally, vertically, or diagonally. They may be read either forward or backward.

ARSONIST	MUGGER
ASSASSIN	MURDERER
BLACKMAILER	PICKPOCKETER
BURGLAR	POACHER
DRUG DEALER	SHOPLIFTER
EMBEZZLER	SMUGGLER
FORGER	THIEF
JOYRIDER	TRESPASSER
LOOTER	VANDAL

```
D A S S A S S I N G S F T N R T
F S A S E A P S E R T S E E H R
F D P H O P L I F T I L H I E C
P I C K P O C K E N G C E G H O
F O R G E R H F O G A R G Y J T
I L Z C R B F S U O E U L L S I
B A R R E L R M P L M Z A S A M
U E E E S A S H G L Z D H M U V
R D L L S C B G O E N O K R R D
G G A Z A K U O B A P C D E I R
L U E Z P M T E V L A E D R N E
A R D E S A E O I L R I Y U O D
R D G B E I G F B E R O H M S R
Z N U M R L T R R Y J T L J R U
D A R E T E K C O P K C I P A M
H V D N R R L J F F R E T O O L
```

Track the Fugitive

The investigator is tracking the fugitive's past trips in order to find and recover information that was left behind in five cities. Each city was visited only once. Can you put together the travel timeline, using the information below?

1. The fugitive went immediately from Australia's capital city to the site of its famous opera house.

2. Adelaide was visited after Melbourne, but not immediately after.

3. Perth was visited before Sydney, but with at least one stop in between.

4. Melbourne was not the second city visited.

5. Adelaide was not the final one.

   Note: None of the cities named so far are Australia's capital city.

Answer on page 360.

DNA Sequence

Examine the two images below carefully. Are these sequences a match or not?

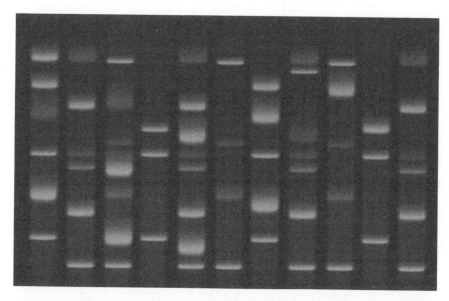

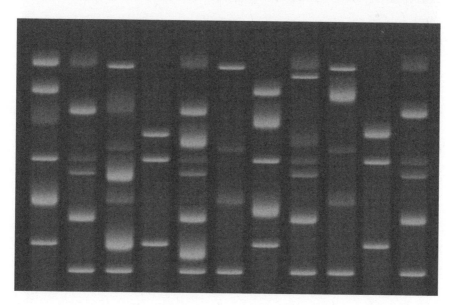

Hostilities of Television

Cryptograms are messages in substitution code. Break the code to read the message. For example, THE SMART CAT might become FVO QWGDF JGF if **F** is substituted for **T**, **V** for **H**, **O** for **E**, and so on.

LTTDRC B UGHPTH ER KTMTWDLDER XBR QTMF IEHO

EVV ERT'L BRKBCERDLUL. BRP DV ZEG QBWTR'K BRZ

BRKBCERDLUL, KQT XEUUTHXDBML IDMM CDWT ZEG

LEUT.

Answer on page 360.

Bank Robbery Alert
(Part I)

A daring mid-afternoon robbery took place today at Paramount Bank in downtown Hadleyville. The following information has been gleaned from eyewitness statements. Read it carefully before turning the page to see how many details you can remember.

Date: Monday, February 15, 2021

Time: 2:09 to 2:14 pm

Suspect description: One female wearing a full motorcycle helmet to cover her face

Approximately 5'6", skin color undetermined, long black hair with purple highlights at the tips. Spoke with a soft Southern accent common to South Carolina, and called people "Sugar" when she spoke to them. Wore a full black leather motorcycle outfit, with gloves, so that no skin was showing. Suspect brandished a Sig Sauer P938, black body with a silver grip, but did not fire it. Emptied two registers and one safety deposit box into a green backpack.

Getaway vehicle: A Harley Davidson Softail motorcycle, silver body with red details and whitewall tires. Georgia license plate began with Z54.

Bank Robbery Alert
(Part II)

(Do not read this until you have read the previous page!)

1. Describe the suspect's hair in as much detail as possible.

_____

_____

2. How many shots were fired during this robbery?

_____

3. In what town did this robbery take place?

_____

4. What color was the suspect's motorcycle?

_____

Answers on page 360.

They Escaped!

The letters in BAILIWICK can be found in boxes 3, 5, 8, 14, 20, 21, and 24, but not necessarily in that order. Similarly, the letters in all these words can be found in the boxes indicated. Your task is to insert all the letters of the alphabet into the boxes. If you do this correctly, the shaded cells will reveal another term.

Hint: Compare ENVIRONS and REGION to get the value of G, then REGION to PRECINCT to get the value of O.

Unused letter: X

BAILIWICK: 3, 5, 8, 14, 20, 21, 24

BOROUGH: 6, 9, 12, 14, 16, 25

DISTRICT: 1, 3, 4, 5, 12, 23

DOMAIN: 5, 6, 7, 8, 11, 23

ENVIRONS: 1, 2, 5, 6, 7, 12, 15

FIELD: 2, 5, 17, 20, 23

JURISDICTION: 1, 3, 4, 5, 6, 7, 9, 12, 22, 23

PRECINCT: 2, 3, 4, 5, 7, 12, 18

QUARTER: 2, 4, 8, 9, 12, 13

REGION: 2, 5, 6, 7, 12, 25

TERRITORY: 2, 4, 5, 6, 10, 12

TOWNSHIP: 1, 4, 5, 6, 7, 16, 18, 21

WARD: 8, 12, 21, 23

ZONE: 2, 6, 7, 19

1	2	3	4	5	6	7	8	9	10	11	12	13
14	15	16	17	18	19	20	21	22	23	24	25	26
												X

The Master Forger

A highly-skilled forger appears to be selling "signed" first edition books all over Escambia County. So far five fakes have been discovered, each sold in a different town for a different price, and each by a different author. Help the authorities track down this miscreant by determining the title and author of each book, the town in which it was sold and its final sales price.

1. The five forged items were the two that sold for $325 and $505, the one sold in Palatka, *By the By,* and *Ends & Means.*

2. Of the two books sold in Ocala and Palatka, one went for $370 and the other was *Caught Inside.*

3. *Ends & Means,* the book sold in Derry, and the book that sold for $325 were by three different authors.

4. The Pam Powell forgery sold for $45 less than the Nick Nells book.

5. Gil Grayson didn't write *Ends & Means.*

6. The Jen Jonson book sold for less money than the forgery that was unloaded at a book shop in West Hills (which wasn't by Pam Powell).

7. The forgery sold in Palatka went for $45 more than the one sold in Micanopy.

8. *At One Time* (which isn't by Jen Jonson) sold for $370.

9. The book by Pam Powell sold for $460.

	Titles					Authors					Towns				
	At One Time	By the Bay	Caught Inside	Dear Deborah	Ends & Means	Gil Grayson	Harry Haupt	Jen Jonson	Nick Nells	Pam Powell	Derry	Micanopy	Ocala	Palatka	West Hills
Prices $325															
$370															
$415															
$460															
$505															
Towns Derry															
Micanopy															
Ocala															
Palatka															
West Hills															
Authors Gil Grayson															
Harry Haupt															
Jen Jonson															
Nick Nells															
Pam Powell															

Prices	Titles	Authors	Towns
$325			
$370			
$415			
$460			
$505			

Building Blueprints

Navigate the twisting path to find your way through this maze.

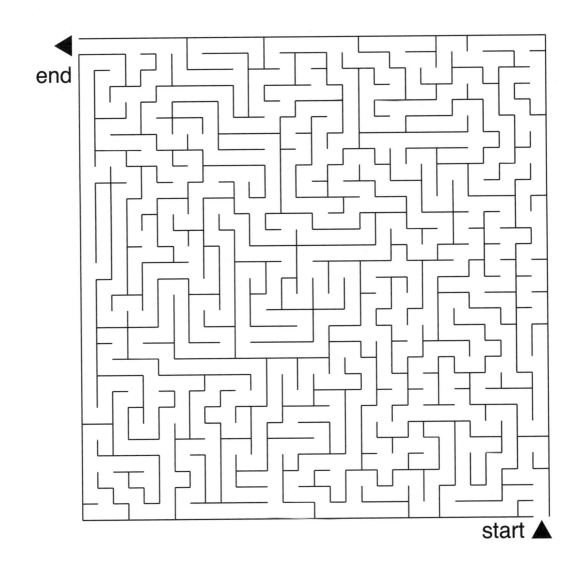

end

start

Answer on page 360.

Motel Hideout

A thief hides out in one of the 45 motel rooms listed in the chart below. The motel's in-house detective received a sheet of four clues, signed "The Logical Thief." Using these clues, the detective found the room number within 15 minutes—but by that time, the thief had fled. Can you find the thief's motel room more quickly?

1. The number is not prime.

2. Neither digit is a prime number (note that the smallest prime number is 2).

3. The number is not divisible by 4 or 7.

4. The number is divisible by 6.

51	52	53	54	55	56	57	58	59
41	42	43	44	45	46	47	48	49
31	32	33	34	35	36	37	38	39
21	22	23	24	25	26	27	28	29
11	12	13	14	15	16	17	18	19

Track the Fugitive

The investigator is tracking the fugitive's past trips in order to find and recover information that was left behind in five cities. Each city was visited only once. Can you put together the travel timeline, using the information below?

1. Madrid and Warsaw were visited back to back, not necessarily in that order.

2. Riga was visited before Zagreb, with exactly one other stop in between.

3. Oslo was either the second or third stop.

4. Warsaw was not the final stop.

Answer on page 360.

Fingerprint Match

Find the matching fingerprint(s). There may be more than one.

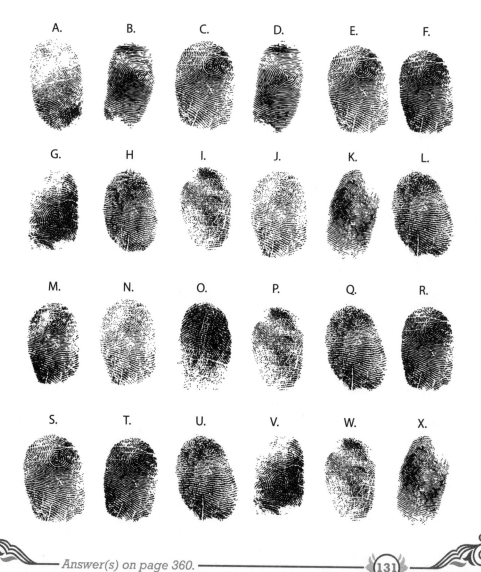

Cybercrime

Every word listed is contained within the group of letters. Words can be found in a straight line horizontally, vertically, or diagonally. They may be read either forward or backward.

BULLYING

EXTORTION

FINANCIAL

FRAUD

HACKING

IDENTITY THEFT

IMPERSONATION

PASSWORD TRAFFICKING

PHISHING

PIRACY

SPAMMING

SPOOFING

SPYING

STALKING

VIRUS DISSEMINATION

WARDRIVING

WEB JACKING

WIRETAPPING

```
G C G I D E N T I T Y T H E F T D F L
B N N U U J X B K I F J O P S N R T S
N O I T A N O S R E P M I H V A J B P
W I K C R N A I H S I H P S U H P J A
I T C K F O P R P U S W I P P E E L M
R A I G N I Y L L U B B G S N Y W O M
E N F O N T N A K V P N B O H I I I I
T I F H A R H A C K I N G U R I M R N
A M A T C O W R N Y S O I E L P N B G
P E R Y P T A W C R K T T E L H G I
P S T T I X R S E S I A S R R P Y K N
I S D I R E D U B P A S P M O C I N
N I R G A M R B N P J O L D A A T V Y
G D O N E W I D N I N A O I H M A X I
U S W E M C V T N A K Y C F K N M Y E
B U S D U P I H T N K L J K I L X I R
R R S I G N I V I R D R A W I N A D V
J I A G J I C N A N I F M T D N G T K
M V P I R A C Y B F V C G H S G G S S
```

A Murderer in the House

Cryptograms are messages in substitution code. Break the code to read the message. For example, THE SMART CAT might become FVO QWGDF JGF if **F** is substituted for **T, V** for **H, O** for **E,** and so on.

TWCK F MVVI FB KWCK FM GRV WCB AGK KG WCHV

C JXUZVU COKXCIIL WCNNVRFRA FR GRV'B WGXBV,

GRV JFAWK CB TVII VRYGL FK, FM LGX SRGT TWCK F

JVCR.

Answer on page 361.

DNA Sequence

Examine the two images below carefully. Are these sequences a match or not?

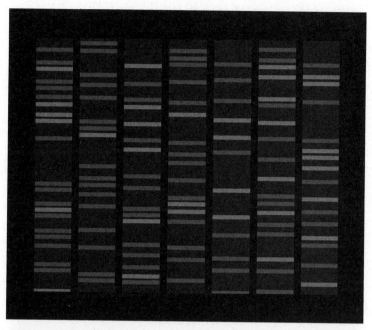

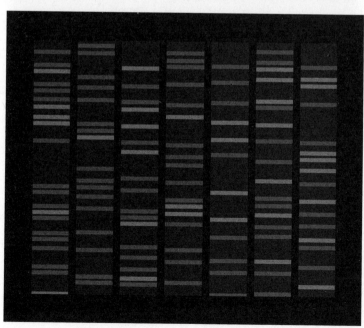

Answer on page 361.

Where'd They Go?

You are tracing the route of a criminal. You know he flew from Miami to Seattle, visiting each city once. You also know he chose the cheapest route for the trip. Can you trace the criminal's steps?

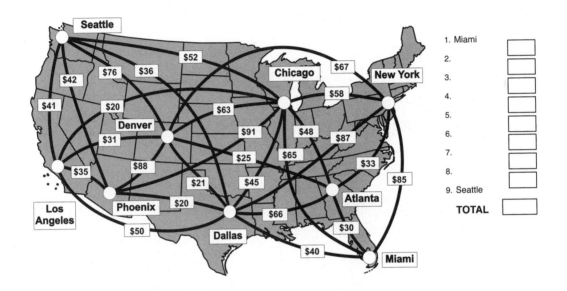

1. Miami
2.
3.
4.
5.
6.
7.
8.
9. Seattle

TOTAL

Answers on page 361.

Bank Robbery Alert
(Part I)

Two banks were robbed this afternoon, apparently by the same duo! The following information has been gleaned from eyewitness statements. Read it carefully before turning the page to see how many details you can remember.

Date: Tuesday, November 9, 2021

Times: 1:43 to 1:50 pm (Bank of Northern Omaha)

2:16 to 2:30 pm (Islington Central Bank)

Suspect descriptions: One male and one female

Male suspect: 5'4", fair complexion with short brown hair and a receding hairline. Wore sunglasses and a bandana around his face. Spoke with a heavy German accent and was referred to twice as "Gunter" by the female. Carried an AK-47.

Female suspect: 5'11", darker complexion, green eyes, with long blonde hair in a ponytail. No facial covering. Spoke with no discernible accent. One suspect thinks she was referred to as "Rita" by the male suspect. No weapon seen in her possession.

Getaway vehicle: An old-style Volkswagen Beetle, baby blue color with Alaskan plates ending in PWR.

Bank Robbery Alert
(Part II)

(Do not read this until you have read the previous page!)

1. How much time passed between the end of the first robbery and the start of the second?

   A. 26 minutes
   B. 16 minutes
   C. 36 minutes
   D. 46 minutes

2. Which of the two suspects was the taller one?

   A. male
   B. they were the same height
   C. female

3. What color was the getaway car?

   A. green
   B. blue
   C. silver
   D. red

4. What name did the female suspect use when addressing the male suspect?

   A. Hans
   B. Stefan
   C. Tobias
   D. Gunter

Answers on page 361.

Motel Hideout

A thief hides out in one of the 45 motel rooms listed in the chart below. The motel's in-house detective received a sheet of four clues, signed "The Logical Thief." Using these clues, the detective found the room number within 10 minutes—but by that time, the thief had fled. Can you find the thief's motel room more quickly?

1. The number is a multiple of 4.

2. The number is not a multiple of 3.

3. The first digit is larger than the second digit.

4. The sum of the digits is 1 less than when you multiply the digits.

51	52	53	54	55	56	57	58	59
41	42	43	44	45	46	47	48	49
31	32	33	34	35	36	37	38	39
21	22	23	24	25	26	27	28	29
11	12	13	14	15	16	17	18	19

Answer on page 361.

Track the Fugitive

The investigator is tracking the fugitive's past trips in order to find and recover information that was left behind in five cities. Each city was visited only once. Can you put together the travel timeline, using the information below?

1. Panama City was neither the first nor the final city on the list.

2. Caracas was either the first or third city.

3. Quito was visited sometime after La Paz.

4. Montevideo is one of the final two cities.

5. From Venezuela, the fugitive went immediately to Ecuador's capital city.

Answer on page 361.

Don't Leave a Print

Change just one letter on each line to go from the top word to the bottom word. Do not change the order of the letters. You must have a common English word at each step.

LEAVE

_____

_____

_____

_____

_____

_____

_____

_____

PRINT

Crime Scene

ACROSS

1. No place for a roller skate
6. Football or badminton
11. One-named author of "A Dog of Flanders"
12. Jouster's protection
13. It's collected at a crime scene
15. Countess's counterpart
16. Ending with Siam or Japan
17. "But of course!"
20. "Naked Maja" painter
22. Sheriffs and marshals, e.g.
24. After-dinner treat
28. "Precious bodily fluid" that may be found at a crime scene
29. Telltale strand that may be found at a crime scene
30. Realtor sign add-on
31. Slangy physician

32. "Good gravy!"
34. It's above the horizon
35. Belonging to the Thing?
38. Metals in the raw
40. They provide a permanent record of a crime scene
45. Font feature
46. Fields of expertise
47. Jets, to Sharks
48. Garment size

DOWN

1. Fastest way to a new lawn
2. Large cask for wine
3. Org. for Saarinen
4. Concept for Colette
5. Devastated
6. "I'm sorry to say..."
7. Canada's Grand ___ National Historic Park
8. Everything: Lat.
9. Fabled giant birds
10. Sequoia or sycamore

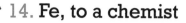

14. Fe, to a chemist
17. Church robes
18. Metaphor for purity
19. Derelict GI
21. Between
23. Pop music's Depeche___
25. Bird of the Nile
26. Giraffe's trademark
27. Homer's besieged city
29. FBI part
31. "CSI" star Helgenberger

33. He was originally called Dippy Dawg
35. ___ dixit (unproven assertion)
36. Back in those days
37. Aching
39. "Love Song" singer Bareilles
41. Bob Cratchit's son
42. Miles ___ hour
43. Crone
44. Direction opposite NNW

Answers on page 362.

Jump on a Train

You're on a runaway train that won't stop moving forward! The path from start to finish must follow the curve of the loops; sharp turns aren't allowed.

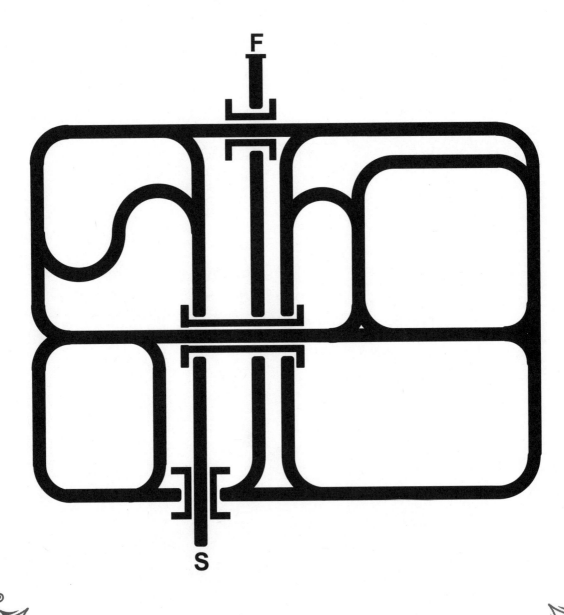

Answer on page 362.

Crime...and Logic

Cryptograms are messages in substitution code. Break the code to read the message. For example, THE SMART CAT might become FVO QWGDF JGF if **F** is substituted for **T, V** for **H, O** for **E,** and so on.

PJKLB KO PQLLQH. ZQSKP KO JUJB. NABJBEQJB KN KO

TDQH NAB ZQSKP JUNABJ NAUH TDQH NAB PJKLB

NAUN RQT OAQTZC CFBZZ.

Interception

You've intercepted two messages. One has the date of a meeting. The other must be the location—but the intercepted list has 13 place names on it. Can you decipher where the meeting is?

THAILAND

ECUADOR

ITALY

YORK, ENGLAND

FAROE ISLANDS

U.S. VIRGIN ISLANDS

TIPPERARY, IRELAND

NIGERIA

NAMIBIA

BIG LAKE

GHANA

OTTAWA

EL SALVADOR

Answer on page 362.

Discover the Alias

The letters in the name ZOE can be found in boxes 4, 17, and 19, but not necessarily in that order. The same is true for the other names listed below. Using the names and the box numbers that follow each name as your guide, insert all the letters of the alphabet into the boxes. If you do this correctly, the shaded cells will reveal another name.

Hint: Look for words that share a single letter. For example, KATE shares only an A with LAURA and only an E with QUEENIE. By comparing the number lists following the names, you can deduce the box numbers of the shared letters.

BETH: 5, 7, 17, 25
BRENDA: 5, 15, 17, 18, 20, 23
CILLA: 21, 22, 23, 24
DAVINA: 15, 16, 20, 21, 23
FRANCES: 6, 10, 17, 18, 20, 22, 23
GLADYS: 6, 12, 14, 15, 23, 24
JOSIE: 1, 6, 17, 19, 21

KATE: 3, 17, 23, 25
LAURA: 13, 18, 23, 24
MARY: 14, 18, 23, 26
MAXINE: 2, 17, 20, 21, 23, 26
PATSY: 6, 11, 14, 23, 25
QUEENIE: 8, 13, 17, 20, 21
WANDA: 9, 15, 20, 23
ZOE: 4, 17, 19

1	2	3	4	5	6	7	8	9	10	11	12	13

14	15	16	17	18	19	20	21	22	23	24	25	26

Whodunits

Every word listed is contained within the group of letters. Words can be found in a straight line horizontally, vertically, or diagonally. They may be read either forward or backward.

BASIC INSTINCT

BIG SLEEP (The)

CHARADE

CHINATOWN

CLIENT (The)

CLUE

D.O.A.

DEATH ON THE NILE

DEEP RED

FALLEN

FRAILTY

GIFT (The)

GONE BABY GONE

GOSFORD PARK

IDENTITY

KISS THE GIRLS

LAST OF SHEILA (The)

LAURA

MEMENTO

MOTHER

MURDER BY DEATH

MYSTIC RIVER

PRIMAL FEAR

PRISONERS

REAR WINDOW

SAW

SCREAM

SEVEN

SUSPECT

THIN MAN (The)

ZODIAC

```
Z  J  V  D  R  J  N  S  K  N  A  T  O  C  F  L  G
E  U  L  C  A  M  Y  B  C  O  K  P  L  R  R  P  O
L  T  N  S  E  Y  L  I  D  R  P  I  A  K  G  B  S
I  F  K  U  F  T  H  G  R  Z  E  I  E  D  H  G  F
N  I  K  S  L  I  O  S  B  N  L  A  Z  L  A  W  O
E  G  N  P  A  T  P  L  T  T  S  U  M  A  A  B  R
H  N  E  E  M  N  S  E  Y  W  S  D  X  S  S  W  D
T  M  V  C  I  E  D  E  E  P  R  E  D  T  L  O  P
N  B  E  T  R  D  A  P  C  T  X  Q  L  O  R  D  A
O  M  S  M  P  I  N  H  H  P  Q  P  S  F  I  N  R
H  I  O  G  E  E  I  I  A  A  E  T  I  S  G  I  K
T  F  D  T  L  N  N  T  R  P  R  P  Z  H  E  W  P
A  U  P  L  H  M  T  Z  A  F  B  U  O  E  H  R  R
E  V  A  R  A  E  R  O  D  Z  F  E  A  I  T  A  I
D  F  O  N  T  P  R  D  E  M  J  B  G  L  S  E  S
P  N  W  O  T  A  N  I  H  C  Z  L  N  A  S  R  O
I  E  N  O  G  Y  B  A  B  E  N  O  G  P  I  N  N
A  G  R  E  V  I  R  C  I  T  S  Y  M  M  K  X  E
M  U  R  D  E  R  B  Y  D  E  A  T  H  X  L  J  R
K  C  U  B  A  S  I  C  I  N  S  T  I  N  C  T  S
```

Track the Fugitive

The investigator is tracking the fugitive's past trips in order to find and recover information that was left behind in five cities. Each city was visited only once. Can you put together the travel timeline, using the information below?

1. From San Diego the fugitive went directly to the other city in California.

2. The fugitive went from Butte, Montana, to Des Moines, Iowa, but not directly. There was a stop in between.

3. Cleveland, Ohio, was one of the first two cities visited.

4. Sacramento was one of the final two cities visited.

5. When the fugitive arrived in Cleveland, it was from the West.

Answer on page 362.

Seen at the Scene (Part I)

Study this picture of the crime scene for 1 minute, then turn the page.

Seen at the Scene (Part II)

(Do not read this until you have read the previous page!) Which image exactly matches the crime scene?

1.

2.

3.

4.

Answer on page 362.

DNA Sequence

Examine the two images below carefully. Are these sequences a match or not?

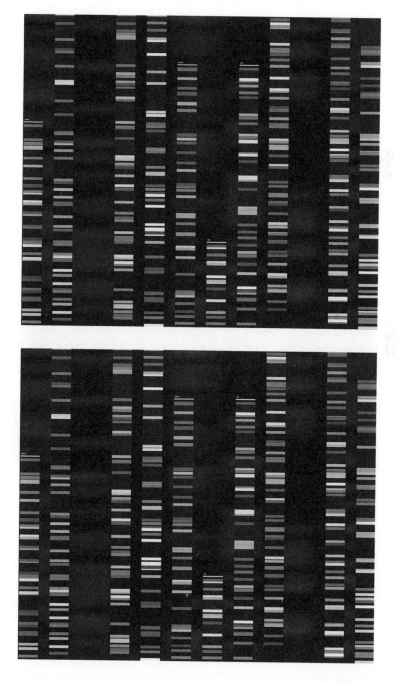

Motel Hideout

A thief hides out in one of the 45 motel rooms listed in the chart below. The motel's in-house detective received a sheet of four clues, signed "The Logical Thief." Using these clues, the detective found the room number within 15 minutes—but by that time, the thief had fled. Can you find the thief's motel room more quickly?

1. The number is odd.

2. The number is not a multiple of 3, nor does it have 3 as one of the digits.

3. The number is prime.

4. The sum of the digits is less than 5.

51	52	53	54	55	56	57	58	59
41	42	43	44	45	46	47	48	49
31	32	33	34	35	36	37	38	39
21	22	23	24	25	26	27	28	29
11	12	13	14	15	16	17	18	19

Answer on page 363.

Bank Robbery Alert
(Part I)

A downtown bank was robbed this morning by two young women. The following information has been gleaned from eyewitness statements. Read it carefully before turning the page to see how many details you can remember.

Date: Saturday, August 9, 2021

Time: 9:46 to 9:55 am

Suspect descriptions:

Suspect #1: 4'11", light-skinned, long brown hair, wore a pink ball cap and dark sunglasses. Carried a small handgun. Spoke softly with a French-Canadian accent and was referred to by the other woman as "Genevieve." She carried out all the stolen money in a green duffel bag.

Suspect #2: 5'10", medium complexion, very short black hair, with purple sunglasses, wearing a T-shirt that said "Texas" on it. Didn't appear to carry a weapon. Witnesses believed she spoke with a Northeastern accent, possibly from Maine or Massachusetts.

Getaway vehicle: A red 1990s Corvette with Arizona plates ending in 5XR. Large dent on the driver's side door.

Bank Robbery Alert
(Part II)

(Do not read this until you have read the previous page!)

1. What day of the week did this robbery take place on?
   - A. Thursday
   - B. Saturday
   - C. Wednesday
   - D. Sunday

2. Which of the two suspects spoke with a Texas drawl?
   - A. the shorter woman
   - B. the taller woman
   - C. neither

3. What were the last three characters on the getaway vehicle's license plate?
   - A. X5R
   - B. XR5
   - C. 5XR
   - D. 5RX

4. Which U.S. state was NOT mentioned in any of the witness reports?
   - A. Massachusetts
   - B. New York
   - C. Maine
   - D. Texas

Answers on page 363.

Couldn't You Be More Like Your Namesake?

Cryptograms are messages in substitution code. Break the code to read the message. For example, THE SMART CAT might become FVO QWGDF JGF if **F** is substituted for **T, V** for **H, O** for **E,** and so on.

H WKQJA NBGHPDSB KY VHSW RNKRFBPP CHV PCB

OHIB JHIB HO CDO YHIKQO NBGHPDKJ, ZQP THO HJ

KQPGHT. CB BORHLBV EQOPDRB DJ 1872, YGBBDJA PK H

NHJRC.

Building Blueprints

Can you escape the scene of the murder? Start at the dot on the left and move to the right.

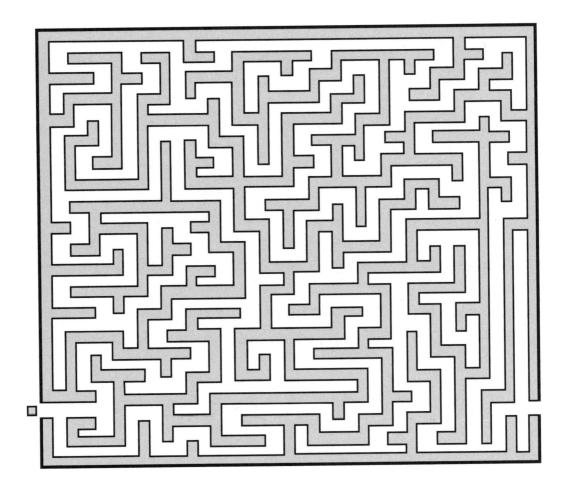

Answer on page 363.

Ways to Get Away

Unscramble each word or phrase below to reveal a word or phrase related to fleeing an investigation.

ON OR FUTON (3 words)

AVIARY DEW (2 words)

DRAIN RITE (2 words)

A PRALINE (1 word)

ADIEU GUSSIES (3 words)

SAUNA AISLE (3 words)

BEGAN OUST (4 words)

BELCHED WIND TORN (4 words)

Answers on page 363.

Missing Words

This word search has a twist. Instead of a list of words to find, we've given you a list of TV show titles with missing words. First, figure out the word(s) missing from each title, then search for the missing word(s) in the grid. Words can be found in a straight line horizontally, vertically, or diagonally. They may read either forward or backward.

1. _____ Most Wanted

2. American _____

3. _____ Nine-Nine

4. _____ & Lacey

5. Crossing _____

6. _____ : Murder

7. Forensic _____

8. Hill _____ Blues

9. _____, P.I.

10. Murder, _____

11. _____ Blue

12. _____ Suspect

13. The _____ Files

14. _____, Texas Ranger

15. Without a _____

```
V B F U C H T Q G U O D S U P
R D Q S T R E E T C Q G I L U
B R E U V H Y F H R J A S D Z
D O P D P Y N S L P X J O U U
A F W K H E H Q R A F O N E T
X K I A M E R I C A S R G R G
M C T K W D M J N B C D A N D
F O L R X E Z G D B Q A I C W
B R O O K L Y N E Z O N D A W
Y T P I B E H W T R A C E A C
E M T L M S Q Q H C B Q L I A
W W M U N G A M P I D K Q L G
E C I T S U J J Z J E S U W N
R F I L E S P W A R R Z D H E
C L S C G T M Z B K H F H P Y
```

The Ponzi Schemers

The SEC is currently investigating five Ponzi schemes masquerading as legitimate hedge funds. Each "fund" was begun in a different year and in a different city, and no two funds have the same total claimed assets. Using only the clues below, match each hedge fund to its headquarters (city), the year it was founded, and the total amount of assets each claims to have under its control.

1. The Alpha Sky fund was founded in either 2007 or 2019.

2. Of the Goldleaf fund and the one with over $200 million in claimed assets, one is headquartered in Seattle and the other was founded in 2019.

3. Both the Wellspring fund and the fund headquartered in Chicago (which are completely separate schemes) were founded sometime between 2005 and 2011.

4. The fund with $105 million in claimed assets was founded sometime after the one headquartered in Los Angeles, but not in 2016.

5. The Wellspring fund, the one based in Seattle, and the one started in 2016 are three different Ponzi schemes.

6. The Gemstone fund, which has more than $200 million in claimed assets, was started three years before the one based out of Miami.

7. The Concorde fund has more than $60 million in claimed assets.

8. The Ponzi scheme based out of Los Angeles doesn't claim to have exactly $50 million in assets.

		Assets					Headquarters					Hedge Funds				
		$32 million	$50 million	$79 million	$105 million	$225 million	Chicago	Dallas	Los Angeles	Miami	Seattle	Alpha Sky	Concorde	Gemstone	Goldleaf	Wellspring
Years	2007															
	2010															
	2013															
	2016															
	2019															
Hedge Funds	Alpha Sky															
	Concorde															
	Gemstone															
	Goldleaf															
	Wellspring															
Headquarters	Chicago															
	Dallas															
	Los Angeles															
	Miami															
	Seattle															

Years	Assets	Headquarters	Hedge Funds
2007			
2010			
2013			
2016			
2019			

Motel Hideout

A thief hides out in one of the 45 motel rooms listed in the chart below. The motel's in-house detective received a sheet of four clues, signed "The Logical Thief." Using these clues, the detective found the room number within 15 minutes—but by that time, the thief had fled. Can you find the thief's motel room more quickly?

1. The sum of the digits is greater than 8.

2. If you multiply the digits, the resulting number is greater than 25.

3. The number is not prime.

4. The number is a square number.

51	52	53	54	55	56	57	58	59
41	42	43	44	45	46	47	48	49
31	32	33	34	35	36	37	38	39
21	22	23	24	25	26	27	28	29
11	12	13	14	15	16	17	18	19

Answer on page 364.

Bank Robbery Alert
(Part I)

An obviously inexperienced thief tried, and failed, to rob the Circle County Bank this afternoon. The following information has been gleaned from eyewitness statements. Read it carefully before turning the page to see how many details you can remember.

Date: Monday, January 10, 2021

Time: 2:45 to 2:49 pm

Suspect description:

White male, mid-20s, 5'6" tall with medium-length blonde hair, a thin moustache and green eyes. Wore thick black eyeglasses and spoke with an Italian accent. Was wearing blue jeans and a black t-shirt with red sneakers. Claimed to have a handgun though several witnesses believed it was a plastic fake. Emptied $1,200 in cash from one register into a grey backpack, but a security dye-bomb exploded soon after, covering him in bright blue paint. Suspect panicked, threw the bag to the ground and ran out the door. A line of blue footprints trailed eastward down Second Street.

Vehicle: Suspect did not leave in a getaway vehicle, though one witness saw him arrive at the bank in a green Ford Taurus with Louisiana license plates ending in WG4.

Bank Robbery Alert
(Part II)

(Do not read this until you have read the previous page!)

1. How much cash was taken out of the bank's register?
   A. $1,2000
   B. $1,000
   C. $2,000
   D. $2,400

2. Which of the following were both green?
   A. eyes and car
   B. t-shirt and shoes
   C. eyes and shoes
   D. car and hat

3. How long was the suspect inside the Circle County Bank?
   A. 2 minutes
   B. 8 minutes
   C. 12 minutes
   D. 4 minutes

4. In which direction did the suspect flee after leaving the bank covered in blue dye?
   A. west
   B. east
   C. north
   D. south

Answers on page 364.

When You Don't Want Your 15 Minutes of Fame

Cryptograms are messages in substitution code. Break the code to read the message. For example, THE SMART CAT might become FVO QWGDF JGF if **F** is substituted for **T**, **V** for **H**, **O** for **E**, and so on.

PDC ORZFCBP KQ PDC SCNW QENOP CLEOKYC KQ

PDC PCHCSEOEKJ ODKT "UICNEBU'O IKOP TUJPCY" EJ

1988, YUSEY FUICO NKZCNPO DEY EJ DEO ULUNPICJP

QKN QKRN YUWO UQPCN OCCEJA DEO BUOC LNKQE-

HCY KJ PCHCSEOEKJ. UIKJA KPDCN BNEICO, NKZCNPO

TUO BKJSEBPCY KQ UNICY NKZZCNW UJY IRNYCN.

Where'd They Go?

You are tracing the route of a criminal. You know he flew from Miami to Seattle, visiting each city once. You also know he chose the cheapest route for the trip. Can you trace the criminal's steps?

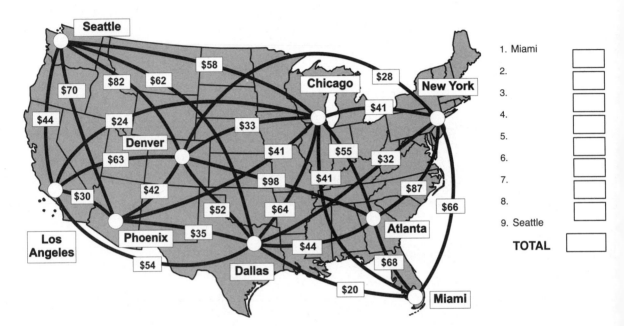

1. Miami

2.

3.

4.

5.

6.

7.

8.

9. Seattle

TOTAL

Answers on page 364.

Fingerprint Match

Find one or more fingerprints that match the one in the box.

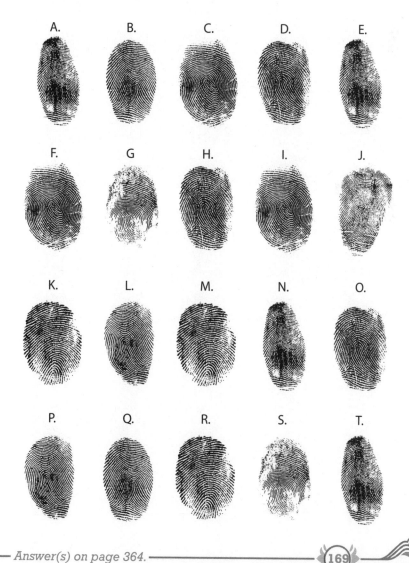

A.　　B.　　C.　　D.　　E.

F.　　G.　　H.　　I.　　J.

K.　　L.　　M.　　N.　　O.

P.　　Q.　　R.　　S.　　T.

DNA Sequence

Examine the two images below carefully. Are these sequences a match or not?

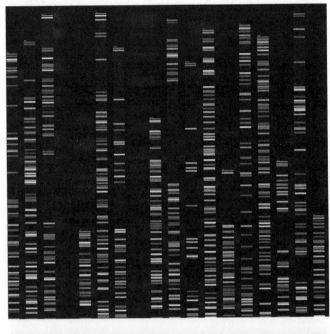

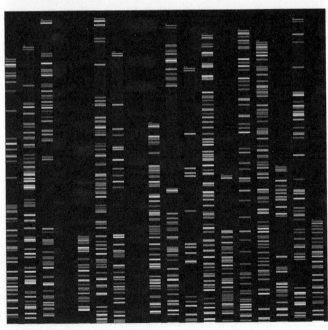

Answer on page 364.

Motel Hideout

A thief hides out in one of the 45 motel rooms listed in the chart below. The motel's in-house detective received a sheet of four clues, signed "The Logical Thief." Using these clues, the detective found the room number within 15 minutes—but by that time, the thief had fled. Can you find the thief's motel room more quickly?

1. The number does not have the digit 3 in it.

2. The digits do not add up to 10.

3. The number is even.

4. Add 5 to the first digit to get the second digit.

51	52	53	54	55	56	57	58	59
41	42	43	44	45	46	47	48	49
31	32	33	34	35	36	37	38	39
21	22	23	24	25	26	27	28	29
11	12	13	14	15	16	17	18	19

Answer on page 364.

A Crime By Another Name

Every word listed is contained within the group of letters. Words can be found in a straight line horizontally, vertically, or diagonally. They may be read either forward or backward.

ARSON

ASSAULT

BATTERY

BLACKMAIL

BURGLARY

CONSPIRACY

CORRUPTION

EXTORTION

FORGERY

FRAUD

HOMICIDE

KIDNAPPING

LARCENY

MANSLAUGHTER

MURDER

PERJURY

RACKETEERING

ROBBERY

TAX EVASION

THEFT

TRESPASS

```
D N Z O P G Y W V A Y R A S S A U L T W K
I O O C U W Z W T R H P N H L T N L P J T
L N M I M L Z C E U G P E R J U R Y Z B H
H C O W T D L T Q L X N T D A I R V P O O
I M N I R P T C O N S P I R A C Y F S S M
Q W E F S A U W T Y F H S P E F D X H C I
C Y F X B A L R R P K O L W P S R M Y G C
T C N N I V E R N N I A A L A P A E H I
R Y Z T E G B E A O P N R Z R T N A U J D
D N R N P B N C X C C K P X M C V D S D E
M S Z A O F E S W A H Z W M H U E K I S M
D O T R L E X T O R T I O N F H Q N O K B
E M J B F G G P O D E X J J J A R D Y L J
B Q Q M L A R K S O C J S Y W M A N A H D
E M A N S L A U G H T E R V O U L C M L Y
N V K Z C N T R B P F H G O Q B K Y F R M
L S Z G T Z A J E U I E E Z J M W Q E O E
R U L P K O J W P X K D C F A B F G S X H
B R A C K E T E E R I N G I T N R K D Q T
B O G Z D Z O L F G S C L K G O L M Q L B
Z H T U R A M U R D E R J D F S Y I Q K Z
```

The Murderer's Itinerary

The letters in ARIZONA can be found in boxes 2, 3, 5, 8, 14, and 16 but not necessarily in that order. Similarly, the letters in all the other cities and states can be found in the boxes indicated. Your task is to insert all the letters of the alphabet into the boxes. If you do this correctly, the shaded cells will reveal another American city or state.

Hint: Compare TEXAS and SEATTLE to find the value of X, then TEXAS to BALTIMORE to find the value of S.

Unused letters: J and Q

ARIZONA: 2, 3, 5, 8, 14, 16

ATLANTA: 2, 3, 19, 23

BALTIMORE: 2, 5, 6, 8, 12, 14, 17, 19, 23

CHICAGO: 2, 5, 7, 8,15, 20

CLEVELAND: 2, 3, 4, 6, 15, 22, 23

FLORIDA: 2, 4, 5, 8, 14, 21, 23

HOUSTON: 1, 3, 8, 11, 19, 20

MILWAUKEE: 2, 5, 6, 10, 11, 17, 18, 23

NEW YORK: 3, 6, 8, 10, 14, 18, 24

OAKLAND: 2, 3, 4, 8, 10, 23

PITTSBURGH: 1, 5, 7, 11, 12, 13, 14, 19, 20

SEATTLE: 1, 2, 6, 19, 23

ST. LOUIS: 1, 5, 8, 11, 19, 23

TEXAS: 1, 2, 6, 9, 19

1	2	3	4	5	6	7	8	9	10	11	12	13

14	15	16	17	18	19	20	21	22	23	24	25	26

Answers on page 365.

Escape from the Park

Can you get away from the murder scene at the park? Start at the top left and make your way to the bottom right.

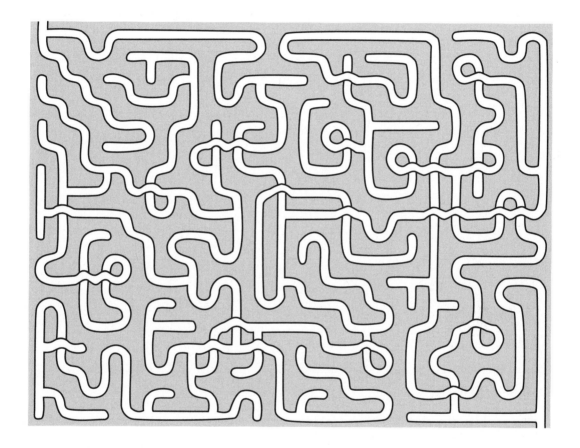

Find the Criminal

Change just one letter on each line to go from the top word to the bottom word. Do not change the order of the letters. You must have a common English word at each step.

LOOK

_____

_____

_____

_____

FIND

Goes Free

Change just one letter on each line to go from the top word to the bottom word. Do not change the order of the letters. You must have a common English word at each step.

GOES

_____

_____

_____

_____

FREE

Answers on page 365.

Interception

You've intercepted a message. You think it might be the location of a meeting between two criminals, but it doesn't seem to make sense. Can you decipher the true message?

AGREED

HOP ROUND SKI LIFT AT HIGHEST ZUCCHINI

RUN AND NEVER GO ON THIN POSTS

VIA ROAD WALK MORE

BANDANNA IN TAN SIDEWAYS CART

READ THE EXCELLENT PAMPHLET

Answer on page 365.

Catch the Suspect

Can you catch the suspect before she finishes getting through the maze?

START

FINISH

Answer on page 365.

Most Wanted Stats

Cryptograms are messages in substitution code. Break the code to read the message. For example, THE SMART CAT might become FVO QWGDF JGF if **F** is substituted for **T, V** for **H, O** for **E,** and so on.

EHLG OWXF 500 IGHIDG WXRG TGGF ZFPDQJGJ HF

OWG DZMO. SWZDG EHLG OWXF 90 IGLPGFO HC

OWHMG DZMOGJ WXRG TGGF PXQNWO, HFDV XTH-

QO 160 SGLG PXQNWO TGPXQMG HC OZIM CLHE OWG

IQTDZP.

They Played Sherlock

ACROSS

1. ___ Rathbone played Sherlock on radio, stage, TV, and film, 1939–53
6. Floating among the clouds
11. "All ___, by the telephone..."
12. One of the simple machines
13. Bitten by a bug
14. Café quaff in Paris
15. Gallic seasoning
16. Holiday threshold
18. $200 Monopoly properties, briefly
19. He played Sherlock on 1938 radio (CBS)
22. Lumber pieces: abbr.
23. Wing, in Paris
24. Apple centers
27. Combats of honor
28. Edgar Rice Burroughs animals
29. Preposition in many Grafton titles
30. He played Sherlock on 1983 animated TV (Australian)
35. Joseph Lincoln book "Cap'n ___"
36. "___ Haw" (rustic TV show)
37. Backside, in French
38. Like the worm-catching bird
40. Kitchen chopper
42. Engine power source
43. Grown-up
44. "Siddhartha" author Hermann
45. Leonard ___ played Sherlock on stage (Royal Shakespeare Company, 1976)

DOWN

1. Deep voice at the opera
2. Put on cuffs, maybe
3. Spiritual essences
4. Homey lodging
5. Tall tales of yore
6. "A Zoo Story" playwright Edward
7. "Hawaii Five-O" prop
8. Blanket
9. Will ___ played Sherlock on film ("Holmes and Watson," 2018)

10. Locks without keys
17. Beetles and Rabbits, for short
20. Beyond chubby
21. Achille ___: hijacked liner
24. Facetious "Get it?"
25. Run, as heavy machinery
26. Stops working
27. Spoiled rotten, maybe

29. Any Hatfield, to a McCoy
31. Squeegee for Luigi, e.g.
32. Creator of a logical "razor"
33. "Hasta ___" ("Goodbye")
34. Kingly title in Spain
39. Word with Cruces or Palmas
41. "___ Ran the Zoo" (Dr. Seuss book)

Track the Fugitive

The investigator is tracking the fugitive's past trips in order to find and recover information that was left behind in five cities. Each city was visited only once. Can you put together the travel timeline, using the information below?

1. Skopje was visited sometime before Stockholm.

2. Riyadh was visited sometime after Seoul, but not immediately after.

3. Dodoma was one of the first three cities visited.

4. None of the cities that start with S were visited back to back.

Answer on page 366.

DNA Sequence

Examine the two images below carefully. Are these sequences a match or not?

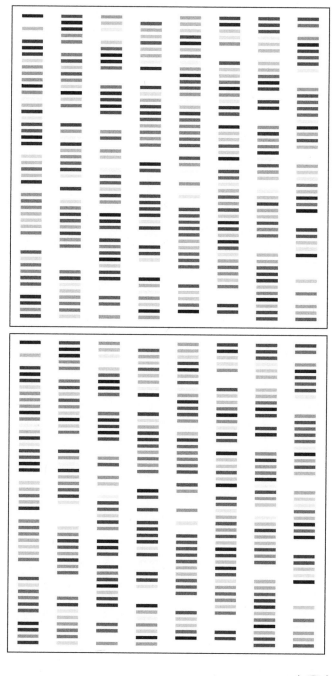

Pinched Paintings

Every word listed is contained within the group of letters. Words can be found in a straight line horizontally, vertically, or diagonally. They may be read either forward or backward.

CHEZ TORTONI (Édouard Manet)

THE CONCERT (Johannes Vermeer)

FEMME ASSISE (Henri Matisse)

LANDSCAPE WITH COTTAGES (Rembrandt van Rijn)

MONA LISA (Leonardo da Vinci)

LE PIGEON AUX PETITS POIS (Pablo Picasso)

PORTRAIT OF A LADY (Gustav Klimt)

POPPY FLOWERS (Vincent van Gogh)

SAINT JEROME WRITING (Caravaggio)

THE SCREAM (Edvard Munch)

SELF-PORTRAIT (Rembrandt van Rijn)

WATERLOO BRIDGE, LONDON (Claude Monet)

```
P S U F S S G L P B R F E B D B L T Z P W
T I I M A E W G Z J Y S R F K M N V D A W
N O P N Z G A Q K R X E H G A V A F B R V
N P S N O A T P J M H H X E V O E J R A P
E S A O K T E C D Q D G R I H Q W P S Y K
P T I N C T R T Q K R C W I E G O I Y Y S
O I N P P O L O J W S Z U L W D L J Q R S
R T T L C C O J T E D D W O T A Y F E H E
T E J X L H O A H Z F B Q M N V O W N I L
R P E K Y T B T O T E E Y O Y U O V T Q F
A X R E H I R T C S M H M G G L K R Y X P
I U O C A W I K P U Y L C M F E E I B X O
T A M S K E D C N A I F U Y E C N X D G R
O N E D M P G X X R E A P C N A W T G H T
F O W N T A E Z Q T F P P O Y L S K Y V R
A E R M D C L P Y E O Q C R R A R S W L A
L G I A E S O Z T P I E T E X Q C G I B I
A I T A I D N X D Z H F J J S F Z W W S T
D P I B A N D N F T G U Q C Y B V R O W E
Y E N P Y A O Q L I K S G R B P K O K C B
H L G E A L N V S B H H T Z Z Z Q H J C A
```

Crime Rhymes

Each clue leads to a 2-word answer that rhymes, such as BIG PIG or STABLE TABLE. The numbers in parentheses after the clue give the number of letters in each word. For example, "cookware taken from the oven (3, 3)" would be "hot pot."

1. The case of the theft of the animal intestines was also called the case of the (6, 5): _____

2. A murder in December (8, 8): _____

3. The lawbreaker who sent hidden messages was the (10, 8): _____

4. To accuse a British "Sir" with a fancy title (6, 6):

   _____

5. A police inspector changes around assignments for the police under him (5, 4): _____

6. To take someone else's breakfast food (5, 7): _____

7. The smuggled dog was also called the (7, 6): _____

8. The incident of theft among the troupe of silent performers was called the (4, 5): _____

Answers on page 366.

Overheard Information
(Part I)

Read the story below, then turn the page and answer the questions.

While on a train, a bystander overheard a criminal tell an accomplice where a set of upcoming thefts would take place. The thief said, "On October 10 we hit the electronics store at Two Oaks Mall, the one on the second floor, not the one near the toy store. On October 12 we've got someone on the inside who will turn off the surveillance video at the jewelry store on the strip mall on 8th and Washington. Then we lie low for a week before hitting the bookstore on Western Avenue on October 20th."

Overheard Information (Part II)

(Do not read this until you have read the previous page!)

The bystander overheard the information about the crimes that were planned, but didn't have anywhere to write it down! Answer the questions below to help the bystander remember what to tell the police.

1. The electronics store is found here.
   A. The first floor at Two Oaks Mall
   B. The second floor at Two Oaks Mall
   C. The strip mall on 8th and Washington
   D. Western Avenue

2. The thieves have an accomplice at this location.
   A. Electronics store
   B. Jewelry store
   C. Bookstore
   D. There is no accomplice

3. The bookstore is found on this street.
   A. Western Avenue
   B. Western Drive
   C. Western Court
   D. Western Street

4. The theft at the electronics place is scheduled for this day.
   A. October 10
   B. October 12
   C. October 14
   D. October 20

Answers on page 366.

Seen at the Scene (Part I)

Study this picture of the crime scene for 1 minute, then turn the page.

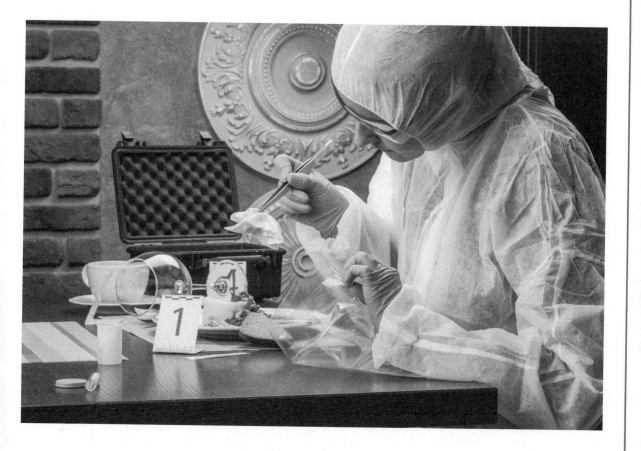

Seen at the Scene (Part II)

(Do not read this until you have read the previous page!) Which image exactly matches the crime scene?

1.

2.

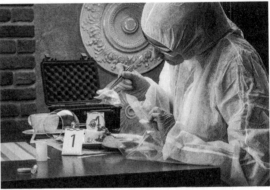

3.

4.

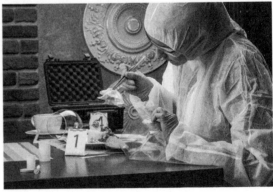

Answer on page 366.

Motel Hideout

A thief hides out in one of the 45 motel rooms listed in the chart below. The motel's in-house detective received a sheet of four clues, signed "The Logical Thief." Using these clues, the detective found the room number within 15 minutes—but by that time, the thief had fled. Can you find the thief's motel room more quickly?

1. The number either contains the digit 9, or the digits add up to 9.

2. If you multiply the two digits together, the result is not greater than 20 but greater than 10.

3. The number is not divisible by 5 or 6.

4. The number is not a cube number.

51	52	53	54	55	56	57	58	59
41	42	43	44	45	46	47	48	49
31	32	33	34	35	36	37	38	39
21	22	23	24	25	26	27	28	29
11	12	13	14	15	16	17	18	19

Answer on page 366.

Mysterious Motive

Cryptograms are messages in substitution code. Break the code to read the message. For example, THE SMART CAT might become FVO QWGDF JGF if **F** is substituted for **T, V** for **H, O** for **E,** and so on.

"FOZN VJ NOB UBZTVTP SG VN, FZNJST?" JZVW OSRUBJ

JSRBUTRC ZJ OB RZVW WSFT NOB MZMBH. "FOZN SY-

EBXN VJ JBHKBW YC NOVJ XVHXRB SG UVJBHC ZTW

KVSRBTXB ZTW GBZH? VN ULJN NBTW NS JSUB BTW, SH

BRJB SLH LTVKBHJB VJ HLRBW YC XOZTXB, FOVXO VJ

LTNOVTIZYRB. YLN FOZN BTW? NOBHB VJ NOB PHBZN

JNZTWVTP MBHBTTVZR MHSYRBU NS FOVXO OLUZT

HBZJST VJ ZJ GZH GHSU ZT ZTJFBH ZJ BKBH."

— NOB ZWKBTNLHB SG NOB XZHWYSZHW YSD

Answer on page 367.

Bank Robbery Alert
(Part I)

A local bank was robbed! The bank has a poster up in its lobby, detailing what they know about the robbers. Read the page, then turn the page to answer questions.

Date: October 15, 2020

Time: 9:45 AM

Suspect description: Male, 6'1", race unknown, hair and eye color unknown

Wore blue vinyl gloves and a mask with red wig and a red mustache and beard attached

Weapon: Ruger LCP II

Getaway vehicle: rust-colored mid-size four-door sedan, possibly a Toyota, model unknown

License plates: Michigan plates, partial number 346 (final three digits)

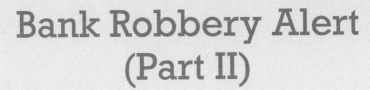

Bank Robbery Alert
(Part II)

(Do not read this until you have read the previous page!)

Fill in all the information you remember.

Date: _____

Time: _____

Suspect description: _____

Weapon: _____

Getaway vehicle: _____

License plates: _____

Answers on page 367.

Track the Fugitive

The investigator is tracking the fugitive's past trips in order to find and recover information that was left behind in five cities. Each city was visited only once. Can you put together the travel timeline, using the information below?

1. Brussels and Moscow were separated by exactly two other cities. Either Brussels or Moscow could have been the earlier visit.

2. Ankara was not the third place visited.

3. Tunis and Athens were visited back to back, but not necessarily in that order.

4. The visit to Athens preceded the trip to Ankara, but not immediately.

5. One of the cities that starts with A was followed immediately by a trip to the city that starts with B.

The Dognapper

Five purebred dogs have gone missing in just the last week, leading some to suspect that a single dognapper is to blame. Each of the five dogs went missing on a different day, and each was of a different breed. No two dogs belonged to the same family. Using only the clues below, match each of the five missing dogs to their breed and family, and determine the day on which each went missing.

1. The Jenkins family found their dog missing two days after the Voigts' dog was taken.

2. The bulldog went missing on either Monday or Friday.

3. The McHales' dog went missing sometime before the Albertsons' pooch.

4. The five dogs were Kenzie, the one that went missing on Thursday, the bulldog and the two owned by the Voigt and McHale families.

5. Of the Great Dane and the McHales' dog, one was Terry and the other went missing on Wednesday.

6. Benji disappeared two days after the Albertsons' dog (which wasn't the Chihuahua) was taken.

7. Sanjay Singh's dog was stolen on Thursday morning.

8. Fido wasn't stolen on Wednesday.

9. Kenzie disappeared one day after the Pomeranian was taken.

	Breeds					Dogs					Families				
	Bulldog	Chihuahua	Great Dane	Pomeranian	Rottweiler	Benji	Fido	Kenzie	Lucille	Terry	Albertson	Jenkins	McHale	Singh	Voigt
Monday															
Tuesday															
Wednesday															
Thursday															
Friday															
Albertson															
Jenkins															
McHale															
Singh															
Voigt															
Benji															
Fido															
Kenzie															
Lucille															
Terry															

Days	Breeds	Dogs	Families
Monday			
Tuesday			
Wednesday			
Thursday			
Friday			

Stolen Art

ACROSS

1. Having to do with bees
6. A little bit of salt
10. 3-Down poet
11. Artery from the heart
12. Breaks in friendly relations
13. Even more adorable
14. First lady's home?
15. "The ___," Edvard Munch painting stolen in 1994 and 2004 and recovered
16. Kilimanjaro's cont.
17. "Annabel Lee" poet
18. '60s campus radical gp.
19. Da Vinci painting stolen in 1911 and recovered in 1913
22. "Hee Haw" honey Misty
23. Legendary puppeteer Tony
26. "___ Bridge, London," Claude Monet painting stolen in 2012
29. Like 7 and 11
32. Cheerless
33. C. Everett Koop and others: Abbr.

34. "The ___," Edgar Degas painting stolen in 2009 and recovered in 2018
36. Gillette razor brand
37. One in a lion cage
38. Larsson who created Lisbeth Salander
39. White poplar tree
40. Richards of women's tennis
41. Island near Venice
42. Congregation's affirmations

DOWN

1. End of "Row, Row, Row Your Boat"
2. Settled in full
3. 10-Across masterwork
4. "This is for," on an env.
5. "Super Mario Bros." console
6. Glum
7. Commedia dell' ___
8. Place
9. Injures
11. Gained entry to
15. ___-disant (self-styled)
17. Hedonist's goal

20. "How cute is that?"
21. Berne's river
24. Author of "Go Eat Worms!"
25. Make eco-friendly changes
27. Brit's "thank yous"
28. Indians or oranges
29. Base-eight system

30. Abu ___ (Arabian sheikdom)
31. Like the Capitol Building
35. Change addresses, in real estate lingo
36. "Up and ___!" ("Rise and shine!")
38. Casa lady: Abbr.

Track the Fugitive

The investigator is tracking the fugitive's past trips in order to find and recover information that was left behind in five cities. Each city was visited only once. Can you put together the travel timeline, using the information below?

1. The fugitive went from Stockholm directly to the capital of Liechtenstein.

2. Vienna and the other city that started with V were neither the first nor last cities.

3. Paris was either the first or fourth city.

4. The trip to Berlin was preceded immediately by a trip to Vaduz.

Answer on page 367.

Fleeing Footwear

The letters in BOOT can be found in boxes 3, 12, and 22 but not necessarily in that order. Similarly, the letters in all the other types of shoes can be found in the boxes indicated. Your task is to insert all the letters of the alphabet into the boxes. If you do this correctly, the shaded cells will reveal the name of another type of shoe.

Hint: Compare MULE and PUMP to get the value of P, then PUMP and MOCCASIN for the values of M and U.

Unused letters: J, Q

BOOT: 3, 12, 22
BROGUE: 3, 4, 10, 12, 16, 18
CHOPINE: 1, 3, 7, 9, 11, 15, 16
GYM SHOE: 3, 4, 5, 15, 16, 17, 24
LOAFER: 2, 3, 6, 10, 13, 16
MOCCASIN: 1, 3, 5, 6, 7, 9, 17
MULE: 2, 16, 17, 18
OVERSHOE: 3, 5, 10, 15, 16, 19

OXFORD: 3, 8, 10, 13, 23
PUMP: 11, 17, 18
SANDAL: 2, 5, 6, 9, 23
SLIPPER: 2, 5, 7, 10, 11, 16
SNEAKER: 5, 6, 9, 10, 14, 16
WEDGE: 4, 16, 21, 23
ZORI: 3, 7, 10, 20

1	2	3	4	5	6	7	8	9	10	11	12	13
14	15	16	17	18	19	20	21	22	23	24	25	26
											J	Q

Name the Novel

Cryptograms are messages in substitution code. Break the code to read the message. For example, THE SMART CAT might become FVO QWGDF JGF if **F** is substituted for **T, V** for **H, O** for **E,** and so on.

CI "QBM HRNYMN JE NJAMN PZFNJVY," QBM ECPIZMM

JE NJAMN PZFNJVY, QBM TCYJTMY HNO. EMNNPNO,

ZJHHCQO ORCZCYM. PZFNJVY QMGGO YN. DPHMO

OBMKKPNY (QBM IJSMG'O IPNNPQJN) QBPQ OBM OMIQ

BCH P ORCZCYM IJQM CI QBM HPCG. OBMKKPNY

CO GPQMN ZPGGMY TBMI PZFNJVY CO HRNYMNMY.

BMNZRGM KJCNJQ CO POFMY QJ ZJHM JRQ JE

NMQCNMHMIQ QJ CISMOQCAPQM QBM ZNCHM.

Bonus: Who committed the crime in the story described above?

Answer on page 368.

Track the Fugitive

The investigator is tracking the fugitive's past trips in order to find and recover information that was left behind in five cities. Each city was visited only once. Can you put together the travel timeline, using the information below?

1. The fugitive did not travel from Austin to Dallas or vice versa.

2. The fugitive traveled to Portland from Nashville, with a stop at one other city in between.

3. The fugitive traveled from one city that starts with D immediately to the next, in alphabetical order.

4. Austin was not the last city visited.

5. Denver was one of the first three cities visited.

Forensic Careers

Every word listed is contained within the group of letters. Words can be found in a straight line horizontally, vertically, or diagonally. They may be read either forward or backward.

ACCOUNTANT	ENTOMOLOGIST
ANTHROPOLOGIST	INVESTIGATOR
BALLISTICS EXPERT	LAB TECHNICIAN
BIOLOGIST	MEDICAL EXAMINER
BOTANIST	NURSE
CHEMIST	ODONTOLOGY
COMPUTER ANALYST	PATHOLOGIST
DENTIST	PSYCHOLOGIST
DNA ANALYST	SCIENCE TECHNICIAN
DOCUMENTS EXAMINER	TOXICOLOGIST

```
Y  P  W  Z  B  Z  P  P  R  D  C  H  E  M  I  S  T
G  K  Q  W  P  A  C  C  O  U  N  T  A  N  T  S  V
O  T  J  I  W  U  A  F  F  U  G  T  G  A  I  L  R
L  M  E  D  I  C  A  L  E  X  A  M  I  N  E  R  E
O  L  A  B  T  E  C  H  N  I  C  I  A  N  T  G  N
T  S  I  G  O  L  O  P  O  R  H  T  N  A  U  T  I
N  P  D  G  N  M  Z  V  O  C  O  Y  E  V  V  J  M
O  V  A  U  H  S  O  R  L  B  J  C  U  V  A  K  A
D  T  R  D  E  N  T  O  M  O  L  O  G  I  S  T  X
O  S  I  N  V  E  S  T  I  G  A  T  O  R  P  J  E
E  S  I  G  Q  F  C  E  S  X  M  U  T  Z  A  A  S
P  S  Y  C  H  O  L  O  G  I  S  T  B  F  K  W  T
R  T  S  I  T  N  E  D  Q  D  G  L  N  G  U  S  N
Z  T  H  I  L  P  A  T  H  O  L  O  G  I  S  T  E
P  K  B  N  U  M  D  N  A  A  N  A  L  Y  S  T  M
T  O  X  I  C  O  L  O  G  I  S  T  B  O  D  N  U
T  K  X  R  Q  U  R  R  I  Z  Z  P  H  U  I  W  C
T  S  Y  L  A  N  A  R  E  T  U  P  M  O  C  B  O
T  R  E  P  X  E  S  C  I  T  S  I  L  L  A  B  D
N  A  I  C  I  N  H  C  E  T  E  C  N  E  I  C  S
```

Motel Hideout

A thief hides out in one of the 45 motel rooms listed in the chart below. The motel's in-house detective received a sheet of four clues, signed "The Logical Thief." Using these clues, the detective found the room number within 15 minutes—but by that time, the thief had fled. Can you find the thief's motel room more quickly?

1. The second digit is larger than the first.

2. The sum of the digits is less than 9.

3. The first digit is odd, and the second even.

4. The first number is greater than 1.

51	52	53	54	55	56	57	58	59
41	42	43	44	45	46	47	48	49
31	32	33	34	35	36	37	38	39
21	22	23	24	25	26	27	28	29
11	12	13	14	15	16	17	18	19

Answer on page 368.

Interception

You've intercepted a message. You think it might be the location of a meeting between two criminals, but it doesn't seem to make sense. Can you decipher the true message?

ABU DHABI

BARBADOS

ARGENTINA

ICELAND

BEIJING

ALBANIA

SOFIA

ANDORRA

GAMBIA

Fingerprint Match

There are eight sets of fingerprints. Find each match.

A.

B.

C.

D.

E.

F.

G.

H.

I.

J.

K.

L.

M.

N.

O.

P.

Answers on page 368.

Find the Witness

On Riverdell Street, there are 5 houses. You need to follow up with a witness, Harriet Chin, but without any address on the doors you are not sure which house to approach. You know from the previous interview that Chin is a single mother with a daughter. The staff at the corner bakery and your own observations give you some clues. From the information given, can you find the right house?

A. The two corner houses are green, while the others are blue. There is a child or children living in one green house and two blue houses.

B. An elderly widower lives alone in the middle house.

C. The nanny for the couple in house E regularly brings her charge by for a treat at the bakery.

D. Sometimes she brings in the daughter of her next door neighbor, but the nanny doesn't like the boy further down the street.

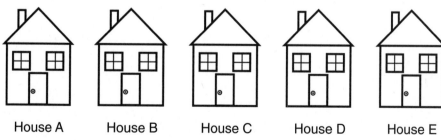

House A   House B   House C   House D   House E

Answer on page 368.

Where'd They Go?

You are tracing the route of a criminal. You know he flew from Miami to Seattle, visiting each city once. You also know he chose the cheapest route for the trip. Can you trace the criminal's steps?

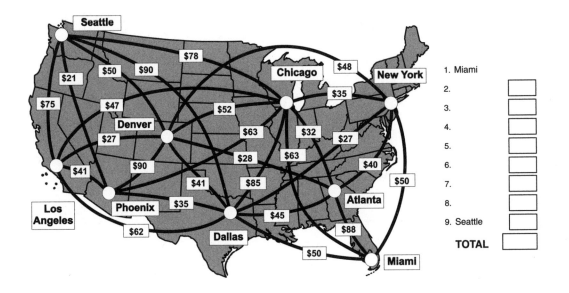

1. Miami

2. ☐

3. ☐

4. ☐

5. ☐

6. ☐

7. ☐

8. ☐

9. Seattle ☐

TOTAL ☐

Answers on page 369.

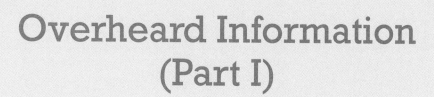

Overheard Information (Part I)

Read the story below, then turn the page and answer the questions.

While on a train, a bystander overheard a criminal tell an accomplice where a set of upcoming thefts would take place. The criminal said, "We're hitting up a bunch of stores on August 12, or August 19 if we do get that heat wave. But if it's under 100, we're still on. This is the order: first the tea shop on Rivers Street, then go to Bakers Avenue for the toy store. Then we ditch the loot at the safehouse on Third Street before going across town to Secondhand Wonders on Fifth Street before going to ground."

Overheard Information (Part II)

(Do not read this until you have read the previous page!)

The bystander overheard the information about the crimes that were planned, but didn't have anywhere to write it down! Answer the questions below to help the bystander remember what to tell the police.

1. The first location will be:
   A. A tea shop
   B. A toy store
   C. A resale shop
   D. An electronics store

2. If there is a heat wave, the thefts will take place on this day.
   A. August 12
   B. August 15
   C. August 17
   D. August 19

3. The safehouse is found on this street.
   A. Rivers Street
   B. Bakers Street
   C. Bakers Avenue
   D. Third Street

4. The resale shop is named:
   A. Secondhand Treasures
   B. Secondhand Wonders
   C. Secondhand Resale
   D. Vintage Treasures

Answers on page 369.

We Still Don't Know Who Done It

Cryptograms are messages in substitution code. Break the code to read the message. For example, THE SMART CAT might become FVO QWGDF JGF if **F** is substituted for **T, V** for **H, O** for **E,** and so on.

DBQ OYIDPL PBLDARQS UYLQ GBRDARQL NKQONL DO

YJNTDJC OJDI NKQ GLYWQAAY LNQTYJN MYJNBQJ

IPLQPI. GB 1990, IQB FDLGBM YL FDAGUQ DOOGUQJL

LNDAQ 13 TDJCL DO YJN TDJNK KPBSJQSL DO IGAAGD-

BL DO SDAAYJL. QIFNX OJYIQL YN NKQ IPLQPI LKDT

TKQJQ NKQ YJNTDJC TYL.

Track the Fugitive

The investigator is tracking the fugitive's past trips in order to find and recover information that was left behind in five cities. Each city was visited only once. Can you put together the travel timeline, using the information below?

1. Rio de Janeiro was one of the final two cities visited.

2. The trip to Lima happened before the trip to Quito, but at least two other cities separated the visits.

3. From Santiago the fugitive went directly to either Quito or Rio.

4. The fugitive did not begin her travels in Buenos Aires.

5. The fugitive did not travel directly from Chile to Brazil.

Answer on page 369.

Crime Rhymes

Each clue leads to a 2-word answer that rhymes, such as BIG PIG or STABLE TABLE. The numbers in parentheses after the clue give the number of letters in each word. For example, "cookware taken from the oven (3, 3)" would be "hot pot."

1. Theft of a sushi ingredient (3, 5): _____

2. Fingerprint found at a cheese store robbery (4, 4): _____

3. Shoplifter from a butcher (4, 5): _____

4. Citrus-related robbery (4, 5): _____

5. Robber of drinks (8, 5): _____

6. Plans to steal boat (5, 4): _____

7. Thoughtful investigator (10, 9): _____

8. Foot impression found in the herbal garden (4, 5): _____

Motel Hideout

A thief hides out in one of the 45 motel rooms listed in the chart below. The motel's in-house detective received a sheet of four clues, signed "The Logical Thief." Using these clues, the detective found the room number within 15 minutes—but by that time, the thief had fled. Can you find the thief's motel room more quickly?

1. The first digit is a prime number.

2. Both digits are even.

3. The second digit cannot be divided by 3.

4. The second digit is not larger than the first digit.

51	52	53	54	55	56	57	58	59
41	42	43	44	45	46	47	48	49
31	32	33	34	35	36	37	38	39
21	22	23	24	25	26	27	28	29
11	12	13	14	15	16	17	18	19

Answer on page 369.

Famous Detective Scramble

The left column contains the scrambled names of five famous fictional detectives. The right column contains the authors who created them. Unscramble the names and then match each detective to its creator!

DETECTIVES:

1. HEMLOCK RESLOSH

2. SLAM SIMPER

3. D. AUSPICE UNTUG

4. FOOL NEWER

5. MONKEY ILLSHINE

AUTHORS:

A. TEX TOURS

B. FORAGES NUT

C. AGHAST CHAIRTIE

D. ADAGE LONER LAP

E. ATRULY HONOR DANCE

Track the Fugitive

The investigator is tracking the fugitive's past trips in order to find and recover information that was left behind in five cities. Each city was visited only once. Can you put together the travel timeline, using the information below?

1. London was the first, third, or fifth city visited.

2. The city in Wales was visited before the city in Scotland, but not immediately before.

3. Neither York nor Edinburgh was the last city visited, but one of them was the fourth.

4. Cardiff was visited immediately before Bath.

5. The visit to York did not immediately precede or follow a visit to London, but it did follow a trip to another city in England.

Answer on page 369.

Seen at the Scene (Part I)

Study this picture of the crime scene for 1 minute, then turn the page.

(Do not read this until you have read the previous page!) Which image exactly matches the crime scene?

1.

2.

3.

4.

Answer on page 369.

Track the Fugitive

The investigator is tracking the fugitive's past trips in order to find and recover information that was left behind in five cities. Each city was visited only once. Can you put together the travel timeline, using the information below?

1. The fugitive began in either Rome or Florence.

2. The fugitive's final visit was to either Florence or Naples.

3. The fugitive went to Milan before Palermo, but not immediately before.

4. The fugitive did not go from Palermo to Naples.

Answer on page 370.

The Wife Poisoner

Severin Kaminski – known in the press as the "Poisoner of Pomerania" – has been implicated in the deaths of five different wives over the last two decades. Each murder took place in a different year and in a different country, and while each murder was done with poison, he never used the same poison twice. Using only the clues below, match up all of Severin's five murdered wives to the year and country in which they were killed, and determine the type of poison he used on each of them.

1. Rebecca was either the wife poisoned with strychnine or the one killed in Canada.

2. The New Zealand murder took place sometime after Annika died of arsenic poisoning.

3. Of Hermione's murder and the one that took place in April of 1999, one involved cyanide and the other happened in Canada.

4. The arsenic murder happened six years after Corinne was poisoned in Mexico.

5. Hermione was murdered six years before Corinne's death, and twelve years before the poisoning in Gdansk, Poland.

6. Severin didn't use nightshade to poison Hermione.

7. Rebecca, who had never been to New Zealand, didn't die in 2011.

	Wives					Countries					Poisons				
	Annika	Corinne	Hermione	Lillith	Rebecca	Austria	Canada	Mexico	New Zealand	Poland	arsenic	cyanide	hemlock	nightshade	strychnine
1993															
1999															
2005															
2011															
2017															
arsenic															
cyanide															
hemlock															
nightshade															
strychnine															
Austria															
Canada															
Mexico															
New Zealand															
Poland															

(Row groups: Years, Poisons, Countries)

Years	Wives	Countries	Poisons
1993			
1999			
2005			
2011			
2017			

Investigative Tools

Every word listed is contained within the group of letters. Words can be found in a straight line horizontally, vertically, or diagonally. They may be read either forward or backward.

AUDIO RECORDER

BARRICADE TAPE

BINDLE PAPER

BIOHAZARD BAGS

BOOTIES

CAMERA

CASTING MATERIALS

CHALK

CONSENT TO SEARCH FORMS

FLARES

FLASHLIGHT

GLOVES

LATENT PRINT KIT

MEASURING TAPE

NOTEBOOK

PAPER BAGS

PLASTIC BAGGIES

RULER

SPRAY PAINT

TWEEZERS

```
E  S  S  T  P  F  H  A  P  A  P  E  R  B  A  G  S
P  Y  L  H  S  G  V  Y  K  M  L  R  M  B  C  S  M
A  V  A  G  T  E  C  B  I  O  E  O  S  C  E  G  R
T  A  I  I  I  G  R  X  R  E  A  T  V  P  S  A  O
G  C  R  L  K  O  L  A  H  K  S  N  U  L  V  B  F
N  B  E  H  T  R  O  O  L  I  R  I  B  A  G  D  H
I  E  T  S  N  S  N  B  G  F  E  A  A  S  J  R  C
R  K  A  A  I  E  L  R  B  P  Z  P  R  T  I  A  R
U  L  M  L  R  I  K  U  P  I  E  Y  R  I  K  Z  A
S  A  G  F  P  T  E  L  S  Z  E  A  I  C  B  A  E
A  H  N  C  T  O  C  E  B  J  W  R  C  B  I  H  S
E  C  I  A  N  O  H  R  N  G  T  P  A  A  N  O  O
M  G  T  M  E  B  G  L  O  V  E  S  D  G  D  I  T
F  A  S  E  T  G  T  A  T  J  I  Q  E  G  L  B  T
S  G  A  R  A  V  L  R  E  G  P  R  T  I  E  V  N
S  X  C  A  L  R  L  Q  B  A  X  Z  A  E  P  Z  E
R  T  Y  V  K  H  F  T  O  T  M  B  P  S  A  J  S
A  G  E  B  V  T  I  S  O  U  U  K  E  B  P  W  N
G  I  C  M  V  D  H  E  K  G  K  H  U  J  E  E  O
R  E  D  R  O  C  E  R  O  I  D  U  A  P  R  A  C
```

The Death of the Party

The letters in BANQUET can be found in boxes 5, 7, 10,, 15, 19, 21, and 22 but not necessarily in that order. Similarly, the letters in all the other party things can be found in the boxes indicated. Your task is to insert all the letters of the alphabet into the boxes. If you do this correctly, the shaded cells will reveal the name of other party things.

Hint: Compare HOSTESS and TOASTS to get the values of A, then FAVORS and FLOWERS for the values of V.

Unused letters: J, X

BANQUET: 5, 7, 10, 15, 19, 21, 22

BUFFET: 7, 10, 12, 15, 22

CENTERPIECE: 1, 3, ,7, 9, 15, 18, 21

DANCE BAND: 1, 5, 7, 10, 11, 21

DOOR PRIZE: 2, 3, 7, 8, 9, 11, 18

FAVORS: 2, 3, 4, 5, 12, 23

FLOWERS: 2, 3, 4, 7, 12, 17, 20

GUESTS: 4, 6, 7, 15, 22

HORS D'OEUVRES: 2, 3, 4, 7, 11, 13, 22, 23

HOSTESS: 2, 4, 7, 13, 15

MUSIC: 1, 4, 9, 22, 24

NOISEMAKERS: 2, 3, 4, 5, 7, 9, 14, 21, 24

PARTY HATS: 3, 4, 5, 13, 15, 16, 18

PUNCH: 1, 13, 18, 21, 22

TOASTS: 2, 4, 5, 15

1	2	3	4	5	6	7	8	9	10	11	12	13
14	15	16	17	18	19	20	21	22	23	24	25	26
											J	X

Answers on page 370.

Track the Fugitive

The investigator is tracking the fugitive's past trips in order to find and recover information that was left behind in five cities. Each city was visited only once. Can you put together the travel timeline, using the information below?

1. From Seoul the fugitive went immediately to Tokyo or vice versa.

2. The fugitive did not go to or from the other U.S. city from Los Angeles.

3. Barcelona was visited sometime before New York, but not immediately before.

4. Los Angeles was visited sometime before Tokyo.

5. Two other cities separated the visit to Barcelona and the visit to Tokyo.

Answer on page 370.

Find the Witness

There are 5 houses on Parson Avenue. You need to follow up with a witness, Danny Boyd, but the paperwork only lists his street, not his specific address. You know from the previous interview that Boyd lives with his girlfriend, and Boyd drives a motorcycle. The staff at the corner bakery and your own observations give you some clues. From the information given, can you find the right house?

A. Couples live in houses A, C, and D.

B. The worker at the bakery counter knows Boyd lives next to a widow, because she used to complain about the noise of Boyd's motorcycle, but now she appreciates that Boyd clears her driveway of snow.

C. The bakery counter worker doesn't know which house the widow lives in, but she adds that the widow doesn't think as highly of the neighbor who lives on the other side of her.

D. Boyd's girlfriend was visiting the couple next door on the day he witnessed the crime.

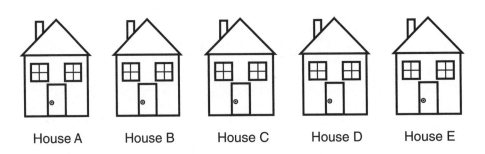

House A   House B   House C   House D   House E

Answer on page 370.

Motel Hideout

A thief hides out in one of the 45 motel rooms listed in the chart below. The motel's in-house detective received a sheet of four clues, signed "The Logical Thief." Using these clues, the detective found the room number within 15 minutes—but by that time, the thief had fled. Can you find the thief's motel room more quickly?

1. The number is odd.

2. The sum of the digits is even.

3. The number is not prime.

4. Add 4 to the first digit to get the second digit.

51	52	53	54	55	56	57	58	59
41	42	43	44	45	46	47	48	49
31	32	33	34	35	36	37	38	39
21	22	23	24	25	26	27	28	29
11	12	13	14	15	16	17	18	19

Quick Crime Quiz

How much do you know about the history of crime scene investigation? Answer the following questions.

1. Long before they were used to identify criminals, fingerprints were sometimes used to "sign" documents in lieu of a signature.

   _____ True

   _____ False

2. In Mark Twain's books "Life on the Mississippi" and "Pudd'n Head Wilson," these were used to identify perpetrators of crimes.

   _____ Hair

   _____ Fingerprints

   _____ Footprints

3. The Bertillion method, named after the French police officer who invented it, used body measurements to establish identity.

   _____ True

   _____ False

4. Bertillion was also the first person to standardize the use of:

   _____ DNA testing

   _____ Mug shots

5. America's first detective agency, the Pinkertons, was created in this year.

   _____ 1850

   _____ 1912

Answers on page 370.

Track the Fugitive

The investigator is tracking the fugitive's past trips in order to find and recover information that was left behind in five cities. Each city was visited only once. Can you put together the travel timeline, using the information below?

1. From Cape Town, the fugitive fled to either Pretoria or Gabarone.

2. Dakar was not one of the first two cities visited.

3. Gabarone was visited immediately before Nairobi.

4. At least one other city separated the visits to Cape Town and Dakar.

5. Nairobi was visited sometime after Dakar, but not immediately afterward.

Identity Parade

Oops! Four mugshots accidentally got sent through the shredder, and Officer Burns is trying to straighten them out. Currently, only one facial feature in each row is in its correct place. Officer Burns knows that:

1. C's nose is one place to the left of D's mouth.

2. C's eyes are one place to the right of C's hair.

3. B's nose is not next to C's nose.

4. A's eyes are 2 places to the left of A's mouth.

5. C's eyes are not next to A's eyes.

6. D's hair is one place to the right of B's nose.

Can you find the correct hair, eyes, nose, and mouth for each person?

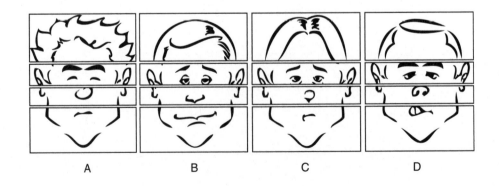

A   B   C   D

Answer on page 371.

Overheard Information
(Part I)

Read the story below, then turn the page and answer the questions.

While on a train, a bystander overheard a woman tell a thief about how best to rob an office. The woman said, "First, you have to promise not to steal any personal stuff from people, just the office stuff. Except from the Director of Marketing, you can take anything from her office, she's mean. They just got new computers for the Sales department, really nice laptops, and those are in the South wing. The CEO has a safe in his office, behind the Monet poster, and the combination is 62-13-21."

Overheard Information (Part II)

(Do not read this until you have read the previous page!)

The bystander overheard the information about the crime that was planned, but didn't have anywhere to write it down! Answer the questions below to help the bystander remember what to tell the police.

1. The woman urges the man to steal from this person specifically.
   A. Director of Marketing
   B. Director of Sales
   C. Director of IT
   D. The CEO

2. The newest laptops on the building are found in this wing.
   A. North
   B. South
   C. East
   D. West

3. The safe is found here.
   A. In the CEO's office, underneath his desk
   B. In the CEO's office, behind a painting
   C. In the CEO's office, behind a poster by Monet
   D. In the CEO's office, behind a poster by Manet

4. This is the combination for the safe.
   A. 62-13-21
   B. 62-21-13
   C. 62-31-21
   D. 62-13-12

Answers on page 371.

Where'd They Go?

You are tracing the route of a criminal. You know he flew from Miami to Seattle, visiting each city once. You also know he chose the cheapest route for the trip. Can you trace the criminal's steps?

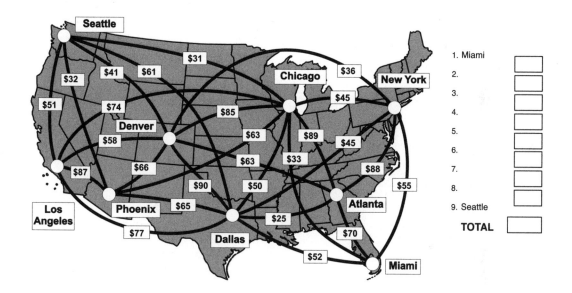

1. Miami

2. ☐

3. ☐

4. ☐

5. ☐

6. ☐

7. ☐

8. ☐

9. Seattle

TOTAL ☐

NYSE Evil Sorcerer

ACROSS

1. Price ___, one of the techniques used in 29-Across
10. North Carolina college town
11. Gift recipients
13. Biblical fratricide victim
14. Portrayer of Jordan Belfort, ___ DiCaprio
15. Gambia money
17. One with a six-yr. term
18. Sheep hassler in the title of a famous Wall Street film
20. Peanut butter cup king
23. Xbox rival
26. To___ (just right)
28. Schwarzenegger's birthplace: abbr.
29. Insider trading, for one
31. International wireless transmission standard for cell phones: abbr.
32. Palm fruit
33. Baseball card stat
35. Cook chestnuts
38. Phishing targets: abbr.
40. Surveillance tool, briefly
42. Proof of who you are
45. Mathematical statement
48. Away from the wind
49. More beloved
50. Nothing, in Spain
51. Intentional deception to secure unlawful gain

DOWN

1. Lark's home
2. Jessica of "Sin City"
3. Year-end time
4. Acquired relative
5. Brouhahas
6. Skin care product
7. Foolish
8. "___ the fields we go..."
9. Homer Simpson's neighbor
12. Small, painful ulcers inside the mouth: canker _____
14. Sang cheerfully
16. Long bath
19. Greek cheeses
21. Freedom from worries
22. Victim of 51-Across, seeking damages in court

24. The Pointer Sisters' "___ Excited"
25. "___ Rock" (Simon & Garfunkel hit)
27. Dines at home
30. Stretch to one's favor, often illegally (as rules)
31. Gordon Gekko in "Wall Street": "_____ is good."
34. Like the Incas

36. Winter neckwear
37. Potato, slangily
39. Hardly enough
41. Sorvino in "Mighty Aphrodite"
43. Jai ___ (Basque sport)
44. Decorate again
46. Math proof letters
47. Abu Dhabi's land: abbr.

The Usual Suspects

Every word listed is contained within the group of letters. Words can be found in a straight line horizontally, vertically, or diagonally. They may be read either forward or backward.

ACADEMY AWARD	KEATON
BARBERSHOP QUARTET	KEVIN SPACEY
BEST SCREENPLAY	KEYSER SOZE
BRYAN SINGER	KOBAYASHI
CHRISTOPHER MCQUARRIE	LINEUP
CON MAN	MCMANUS
DAVE KUJAN	MR. HOCKNEY
ENSEMBLE	MYSTERY
FENSTER	SAN PEDRO
HEIST	VERBAL

```
C R H E I S N O T A E K U I S T E V D N
Z H B A R B E R S H O P Q U A E C E M B
V M R H O C K N E Y M N O C Y T K R C R
H Q Y I O W Y C O N M A N M A R R B M E
M R I A S R S E E N I L U Y B A E A A V
S U J C L T D V C I B Z D S O U Z L N T
A S U A G P O E F A I O P T K Q O B C S
N U K D K B N P P I P W C E L P S F P I
P N E E A M M E H N H S T R H O R U N E
E A V M Y V K E E E A S N Y J H E H E H
D M A Y P S E R S R R S A I B S S M E I
K C D A K U E K B N C M U Y V R Y R R P
E M O W N V E R U G E S C R A E E H C E
V T R A O F Y N S J T L T Q M B K O S L
I A B R M A M Y I O A G G S U R O C T B
N E R D N Y U N O L W N T A E A Y K S M
S K U S S R E G N I S N A Y R B R N E E
P N I T K E C E W A Y M E D A C A R B S
A N E T S N E F R E T S N E F I U T I N
A U Q C M R E H P O T S I R H C U W Q E
```

Track the Fugitive

The investigator is tracking the fugitive's past trips in order to find and recover information that was left behind in five cities. Each city was visited only once. Can you put together the travel timeline, using the information below?

1. The visit to Mexico City came direclty between the visits to the two Canadian cities.

2. Copenhagen was one of the first two cities visited.

3. Ottawa was visited immediately before the other city that began with O.

4. Toronto was visited sometime before Oslo.

Answer on page 371.

Motel Hideout

A thief hides out in one of the 45 motel rooms listed in the chart below. The motel's in-house detective received a sheet of four clues, signed "The Logical Thief." Using these clues, the detective found the room number within 15 minutes—but by that time, the thief had fled. Can you find the thief's motel room more quickly?

1. The number is even.

2. The sum of the digits is odd.

3. Either the number 4 is one of the digits or the number is divisible by 4, but not both.

4. The sum of the digits is greater than 10.

51	52	53	54	55	56	57	58	59
41	42	43	44	45	46	47	48	49
31	32	33	34	35	36	37	38	39
21	22	23	24	25	26	27	28	29
11	12	13	14	15	16	17	18	19

Answer on page 372.

On the Culprit's Trail

ACROSS

1. Big jets
6. Ethylene alcohol
11. Not at hand
12. CBS forensic drama, for short
14. Words of worry
15. Shake, as a police tail
16. Domestic fowl
17. "The ___ Medieval" (2011 video game)
18. It might be marked off with police tape
20. Rotunda's crown
21. Gardener's need
25. Bumps and thumps in the night
30. Detective's job
32. Casts out
33. Showing strain
34. What some hockey games end in
37. William Petersen's character on hit CBS series
41. Mega- or giga- ending
42. Hoppy brew
43. Put in a hot oven
45. Swamp snapper
46. Department of Defense code-breaking org.
47. ___ and terminer (high criminal court)
48. Bassoon starter
49. Empties, with "out"

DOWN

1. Shutter
2. Strange sighting in the night sky
3. Not fem.
4. Informal title before a man's name, from brother
5. Joe ___ (average guy)
6. Healthy root
7. Park in California
8. Goatee spot
9. 'This one's ___'
10. Start of many California town names
13. Have the look
19. That is (Latin)
22. Web image file format
23. Madison or Pennsylvania: abbr.

24. Cancel a choice
26. Writer Joyce Carol ___
27. Stray from righteousness
28. Daughter of Helios
29. Gym wear
31. Russian empress
35. Bill additions
36. Sci-fi's Asimov
37. Sandwich served with tzatziki

38. Marvin Gaye's "Let's Get ___"
39. Clarinet kin
40. Ancient Mexican pyramid builders
41. Include secretly, as in an email exchange
44. Classic Mattel doll

The Embezzler

Courtney Crunk, a high-powered executive who has worked at a number of different Fortune 500 companies over the last decade, is suspected to have embezzled large sums of money from five of her most recent employers. Help the federal prosecutor build a case against Courtney by determining how much money she stole from each of these five companies, and match each of those companies to its location and industry.

1. The five companies are: Centrafour, the one that reported $2 million in embezzled funds, and the three companies in telephony, logistics and web hosting.

2. Of Dynacorp and the company based out of New York, one is focused on logistics and the other reported $2 million in embezzled funds.

3. The mobile app company lost more money than Melcisco.

4. The company based out of Portland is either the one that lost $1 million or Dynacorp.

5. Courtney Crunk stole either $1 million or $8 million from the microchip manufacturer over a period of nine months.

6. Centrafour isn't headquartered in Chicago.

7. The company based in Atlanta lost half as much money as Wexica Incorporated.

8. Of Melcisco and the company based in Portland, one is focused on web hosting and the other reported $4 million stolen in 2020.

9. Courtney didn't steal exactly $1 million from the Atlanta company.

		Companies					Locations					Industries				
		Centrafour	Dynacorp	Melcisco	Truetel	Wexica Inc.	Atlanta	Boston	Chicago	New York	Portland	logistics	microchips	mobile apps	telephony	web hosting
Amounts	$500,000															
	$1,000,000															
	$2,000,000															
	$4,000,000															
	$8,000,000															
Industries	logistics															
	microchips															
	mobile apps															
	telephony															
	web hosting															
Locations	Atlanta															
	Boston															
	Chicago															
	New York															
	Portland															

Amounts	Companies	Locations	Industries
$500,000			
$1,000,000			
$2,000,000			
$4,000,000			
$8,000,000			

Answers on page 372.

Fictional Medical Examiners

Every word listed is contained within the group of letters. Words can be found in a straight line horizontally, vertically, or diagonally. They may be read either forward or backward.

AL ROBBINS (CSI: Crime Scene Investigation)
ALEXX WOODS (CSI: Miami)
CAMILLE SAROYAN (Bones)
DAVID PHILLIPS (CSI: Crime Scene Investigation)
ELIZABETH RODGERS (Law and Order franchise)
EVE LOCKHART (Waking the Dead)
FELIX GIBSON (Waking the Dead)
FRANKIE WHARTON (Waking the Dead)
GERALD JACKSON (NCIS)
JIMMY PALMER (NCIS)
JORDAN CAVANAUGH (Crossing Jordan)
JULIANNA COX (Homicide)
KAY SCARPETTA (Patricia Cornwell's book series)
LORETTA WADE (NCIS: New Orleans)
MAURA ISLES (Rizzoli and Isles)
MAX BERGMAN (Hawaii Five-O)
MELINDA WARNER (Law and Order: SVU)
QUINCY (Quincy, M.E.)
ROSE SCHWARTZ (NCIS: Los Angeles)

```
L M K C A M I L L E S A R O Y A N
N O S N K A Y S C A R P E T T A D
O F R E N O S K C A J D L A R E G
T O T E L X O C A N N A I L U J Y
R R A G T S F Y F L E K Z D P C C
A L A L L T I M S Q V J A U G M H
H L W H H Q A A A B G X B F S E G
W N E A K B U W R X K H E E P L U
E P P X B C F I A U B R T L V I A
I N Y E X P O P N D A E H I X N N
K Z U R W W Q L M C E M R X G D A
N A J H I N O T E P Y L O G F A V
A L B O N Y E O Q V S A D I M W A
R R E T O A K N D A E P G B M A C
F O D E E X G C O S H Y E S D R N
J B C S Z X G E G O Y M R O Q N A
S B L P H W E I M V Y M S N D E D
Y I S P I L L I H P D I V A D R R
T N P G J D Q P Q R O J F D X B O
Y S Q R O S E S C H W A R T Z L J
```

Describe the Criminal's Hairdo

The letters in BANGS can be found in boxes 3, 6, 14, 18, and 20 but not necessarily in that order. Similarly, the letters in all the other hairdos can be found in the boxes indicated. Your task is to insert all the letters of the alphabet into the boxes. If you do this correctly, the shaded cells will reveal the name of another hairdo.

Hint: Compare PONYTAIL and PIGTAIL to get the value of G, then BUN and BANGS for the value of U.

Unused letters, J, Q, and X

BANGS: 3, 6, 14, 18, 20
BEEHIVE: 4, 8, 14, 17, 19
BOUFFANT: 3, 5, 10, 12, 14, 15, 18
BRAIDS: 3, 4, 6, 9, 14, 21
BUN: 10, 14, 18
CHIGNON: 4, 12, 16, 17, 18, 20
CURLS: 2, 6, 9, 10, 16
FRIZZ: 4, 9, 11, 15
MARCEL WAVE: 2, 3, 8, 9, 13, 16, 19, 22

PAGEBOY: 1, 3, 8, 12, 14, 20, 23
PERMANENT: 1, 3, 5, 8, 9, 13, 18
PIGTAIL: 1, 2, 3, 4, 5, 20
PONYTAIL: 1, 2, 3, 4, 5, 12, 18, 23
RINGLETS: 2, 4, 5, 6, 8, 9, 18, 20
TOPKNOT: 1, 5, 7, 12, 18

1	2	3	4	5	6	7	8	9	10	11	12	13
14	15	16	17	18	19	20	21	22	23	24	25	26
										J	Q	X

Answers on page 372.

Bank Robbery Alert
(Part I)

A local bank was robbed! The bank has a poster up in its lobby, detailing what they know about the robbers. Read the page, then turn the page to answer questions.

Date: January 8, 2021

Time: 2:17 to 2:33 PM

Suspect description:

White male, 5'10", short brown hair, eye color unknown, wore a mask over the lower part of his face

White female, 5'5", shoulder-length layered brown hair, eye color unknown, wore sunglasses and a mask over the lower part of her face

A third suspect, description unknown, drove the getaway vehicle

Names: Male robber referred to woman as "Darling," and "Sweet Lily"

Weapons: Machine guns

Getaway vehicle: small-size SUV, black, license plates unknown

Bank Robbery Alert
(Part II)

(Do not read this until you have read the previous page!)

Fill in all the information you remember.

Date: _____

Time: _____

Suspect descriptions:

Suspect 1: _____
_____

Suspect 2: _____
_____

Suspect 3: _____
_____

Names: _____

Weapons: _____

Getaway vehicle: _____

Answers on pages 372/373.

Track the Fugitive

The investigator is tracking the fugitive's past trips in order to find and recover information that was left behind in five cities. Each city was visited only once. Can you put together the travel timeline, using the information below?

1. The two Great Lakes cities were not visited one after the other.

2. Atlanta was either the first or last city visited.

3. Chicago was visited sometime after Pittsburgh.

4. From Milwaukee, the fugitive went directly to the city in Florida.

5. Tampa was visited sometime before Pittsburgh.

6. At least one other city separates the visits between Atlanta and Chicago.

Answer on page 373.

Motel Hideout

A thief hides out in one of the 45 motel rooms listed in the chart below. The motel's in-house detective received a sheet of four clues, signed "The Logical Thief." Using these clues, the detective found the room number within 15 minutes—but by that time, the thief had fled. Can you find the thief's motel room more quickly?

1. The first digit is equal to or smaller than the second digit.

2. The sum of the digits is less than 10.

3. The number is divisible by 4 but not 3.

4. The digits add up to an even number.

51	52	53	54	55	56	57	58	59
41	42	43	44	45	46	47	48	49
31	32	33	34	35	36	37	38	39
21	22	23	24	25	26	27	28	29
11	12	13	14	15	16	17	18	19

Answer on page 373.

Seen at the Scene (Part I)

Study this picture of the crime scene for 1 minute, then turn the page.

Seen at the Scene (Part II)

(Do not read this until you have read the previous page!)

Which image exactly matches the crime scene?

1.

2.

3.

4.

Answer on page 373.

Find the Witness

On Persimmon Street, there are 5 houses. You need to gather a witness statement from Anjali Patel, but without any address on the doors you are not sure which house to approach. You know that Patel is a single woman who lives by herself. The staff at the coffee shop around the corner and your own observations give you some clues. From the information given, can you find the right house?

A. One member of the wait staff says Ms. Patel lives at one of the two green houses on the street.

B. Another member of the wait staff knows that a family lives in house C.

C. House D is yellow.

D. The house at one end of the street is blue; the house at the other end is white.

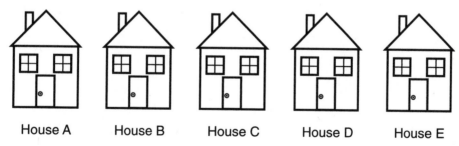

House A   House B   House C   House D   House E

Answer on page 373.

Track the Fugitive

The investigator is tracking the fugitive's past trips in order to find and recover information that was left behind in five cities. Each city was visited only once. Can you put together the travel timeline, using the information below?

1. The fugitive neither began nor ended his journey in Johannesburg.

2. Rio de Janeiro was visited either immediately before or immediately after New York.

3. Law enforcement almost caught the fugitive in Jakarta, but he took the first flight out to Perth.

4. Johannesburg was visited sometime after Perth.

5. From South Africa, the fugitive went immediately to South America.

Answer on page 373.

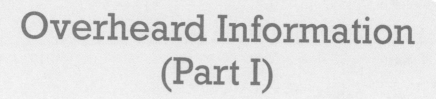

Overheard Information (Part I)

Read the story below, then turn the page and answer the questions.

While on a train, a bystander overheard a woman tell a man about how best to rob a museum. The woman said, "They have two security guards monitoring the tapes, but one takes a half-hour break at 12:30 am and the other has been paid off. I'm going to leave a window open in the South side of the building, near the pottery exhibit. From there you just have to go through the guard's passageway to get to the gemstone exhibit. But remember, if you get caught and implicate me, I'm going to give evidence against you—and I have your fingerprints all over two artifacts from 2016."

Overheard Information (Part II)

(Do not read this until you have read the previous page!)

The bystander overheard the information about the crime that was planned, but didn't have anywhere to write it down! Answer the questions below to help the bystander remember what to tell the police.

1. The thieves mention two exhibits.
   A. Masks and gems
   B. Pottery and gems
   C. Gems and artifacts
   D. Pottery and masks

2. One of the thieves was involved in an art theft in this year.
   A. 2016
   B. 2012
   C. 2016
   D. 2018

3. How many security guards will be on duty?
   A. At least two
   B. At least three
   C. Four
   D. Only one

4. The unlocked window will be found in this wing.
   A. South
   B. West
   C. East
   D. Basement

Answers on page 373.

Motel Hideout

A thief hides out in one of the 45 motel rooms listed in the chart below. The motel's in-house detective received a sheet of four clues, signed "The Logical Thief." Using these clues, the detective found the room number within 15 minutes—but by that time, the thief had fled. Can you find the thief's motel room more quickly?

1. Each digit is either a prime number or 1.

2. The number itself is not prime.

3. The second digit is larger than the first.

4. Add the digits together, and the result is divisible by both 3 and 4.

51	52	53	54	55	56	57	58	59
41	42	43	44	45	46	47	48	49
31	32	33	34	35	36	37	38	39
21	22	23	24	25	26	27	28	29
11	12	13	14	15	16	17	18	19

Answer on page 373.

Deadly Perfume

ACROSS

1. What the title villain of this puzzle obsessed about
10. Oil can letters
11. Gobble
12. Country with capital city Port-au-Prince
13. Pencil tops
15. Bermuda hrs.
16. Cruel Roman emperor
17. Like the sight of the title perfume maker's private laboratory
19. Migraine precursors
21. Loughlin of "Full House"
24. Graduates-to-be: abbr.
25. Yellowish-green Eurasian finch
27. Maker of frozen potato-based foods, ___-Ida
29. Per Ben Franklin,   "Nothing is certain except ____ and taxes."
31. Wiper
32. Campaign supporter
34. Docs' group

36. Meyers of "Saturday Night Live"
37. Part of WTO
40. Mountain nymph
42. Bygone Russian ruler
45. Ending for Japan
46. Bedgown
48. Flood prevention barrier
49. Hamburger's home: abbr.
50. Citrus drink suffix
51. Very old French technique of extracting the aromatic oils from flowers

DOWN

1. Cabbie's passenger
2. Back section
3. 'Golly!'
4. Pinker inside
5. On a cruise
6. Beverage that is a blend of black tea, honey, spices, and milk
7. Three-legged stands
8. Warm a bench
9. Series of murders in a short amount of time

10. One of the five that allows humans to detect and en joy odors
14. Fly high, as an eagle
18. Take a coffee break
20. Food pyramid org.
22. Gumbo veggie
23. Fjord cousin
24. Paving stone (var.)
26. '___ no idea!'
28. Charlotte of "The Facts of Life"
30. Suffix with maison or kitchen

33. Selected to become the next victim
35. Illicit drug made in labs
38. Cowboy's home
39. French farewell
41. Lagoon barrier
43. Party without women
44. White House operative
45. Poetic dusk
47. Growl of anger or disappointment

Crime Rhymes

Each clue leads to a 2-word answer that rhymes, such as BIG PIG or STABLE TABLE. The numbers in parentheses after the clue give the number of letters in each word. For example, "cookware taken from the oven (3, 3)" would be "hot pot."

1. Suspect swore he was getting fast food (3, 5): _____

2. Arsonist who hated musical instruments set this (4, 4): _____

3. Murder at the racetrack (12, 4): _____

4. Cantaloupe thief (5, 5): _____

5. Scoff at idea of using this poison (5, 7): _____

6. Provided poison (8, 7): _____

7. Noisy diamond heist (3, 6): _____

8. When the funeral home thought something might be going on (9, 9): _____

Answers on page 374.

Come Together

Set each of the tile sets into the empty spaces below to create 3 nine-letter words related to investigation. Each tile set is used only once.

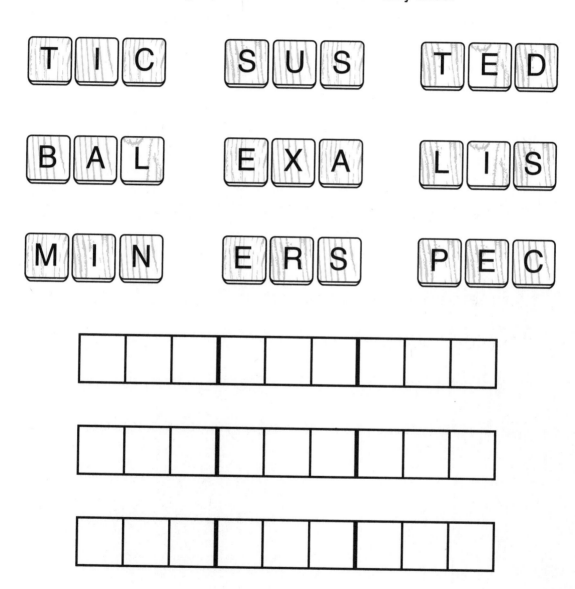

 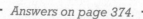

Codes and Ciphers

Every word listed is contained within the group of letters. Words can be found in a straight line horizontally, vertically, or diagonally. They may be read either forward or backward.

ALGORITHM

BLOCK

CAESAR SHIFT

CODE

CIPHERTEXT

CRYPTANALYST

CRYPTOGRAM

DECRYPTION

ENCRYPTION

HIDDEN

KEY

PLAINTEXT

STREAM

SUBSTITUTION

TRANSPOSITION

VIGENÈRE

```
S  U  B  S  T  I  T  U  T  I  O  N  F  P  N
G  I  C  R  Y  P  T  A  N  A  L  Y  S  T  O
C  N  I  R  U  Y  O  J  N  K  C  Q  Q  N  I
A  O  P  Z  E  B  Q  E  F  S  C  V  Q  Z  T
E  I  H  K  D  L  C  Z  T  M  N  O  P  W  P
S  T  E  M  Q  R  B  R  H  M  U  L  L  U  Y
A  I  R  N  G  V  E  T  A  P  A  X  H  B  R
R  S  T  H  C  A  I  R  H  I  D  D  E  N  C
S  O  E  X  M  R  G  G  N  L  J  R  N  L  E
H  P  X  Q  O  O  Y  T  E  B  U  U  S  Z  D
I  S  T  G  T  F  E  P  S  N  P  Q  M  C  C
F  N  L  P  H  X  Q  N  T  L  È  M  K  O  P
T  A  Y  Q  T  B  N  Q  E  I  T  R  D  X  G
J  R  M  L  A  J  C  Z  U  S  O  E  E  Z  G
C  T  A  Z  U  M  X  D  Q  P  M  N  B  E  L
```

Identity Parade

Mrs. Amnesia was asked to recollect the faces of the 4 suspects who robbed the local bank. Her memory is a bit shaky though. The photos accidentally got put through a shredder, and, currently, only one facial feature in each row is in its correct place. Mrs. Amnesia does know that:

1. B's nose is not next to C's nose.

2. B's hair is one place to the right of B's nose.

3. B's eyes are one place to the right of B's mouth.

4. A's hair is one place to the left of D's mouth.

5. B's eyes are not on the same face as C's nose.

6. C's eyes are one place to the left of C's nose.

Can you find the correct hair, eyes, nose, and mouth for each suspect?

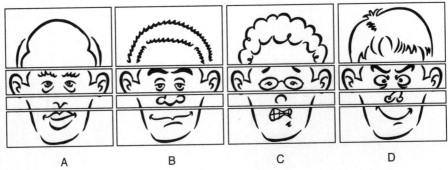

A   B   C   D

Answer on page 374.

Track the Fugitive

The investigator is tracking the fugitive's past trips in order to find and recover information that was left behind in five cities. Each city was visited only once. Can you put together the travel timeline, using the information below?

1. From Paris, the fugitive went directly to the other capital city in Europe.

2. Seoul was not the last city visited.

3. Buenos Aires was visited sometime before, but not immediately before, Prague.

4. Cairo was one of the first three cities visited, but not the first.

5. From Asia, the fugitive went directly to South America.

Where'd They Go?

You are tracing the route of a criminal. You know he flew from Miami to Seattle, visiting each city once. You also know he chose the cheapest route for the trip. Can you trace the criminal's steps?

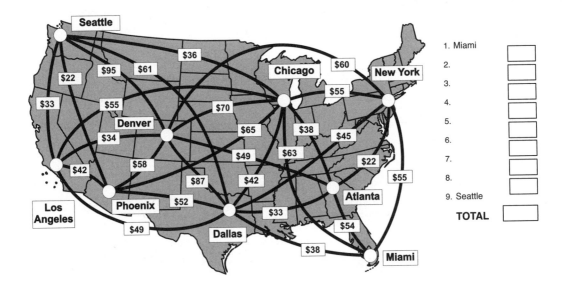

1. Miami
2.
3.
4.
5.
6.
7.
8.
9. Seattle
TOTAL

Answers on page 374.

Overheard Information (Part I)

Read the story below, then turn the page and answer the questions.

While on a train, a bystander overheard a conversation between a man and a woman talking about how best to rob an antique store.

The woman says, "They lock up their money in the safe each night, and Jorie's given me the combo. 06-41-18. They go to the bank every Wednesday. They don't open until 10 AM and they never arrive themselves before 8, so let's go Wednesday before they open, about 6 AM."

The man says, "I've scoped out the video situation. They don't use their cameras to record—they just have them there to deter robberies. But the store on the left, the art gallery, have a camera on the front sidewalk—so we have to approach and leave from the back."

Overheard Information (Part II)

(Do not read this until you have read the previous page!)

1. Which statement about the overheard conversation is true?
   A. The conversation was between a man and a woman, and the woman spoke first.
   B. The conversation was between a man and a woman, and the man spoke first.
   C. The conversation was between two men.
   D. The conversation was between two women.

2. The combo for the safe is:
   A. 66-41-18
   B. 60-41-18
   C. 06-41-18
   D. 06-14-18

3. The theft is planned for this day and time.
   A. Tuesday about 6 PM
   B. Wednesday around 6 AM
   C. Wednesday around 8 AM
   D. Wednesday around 10 AM

4. The name of the accomplice who gave the safe code is:
   A. Jorie
   B. Joey
   C. Jordy
   D. Jolie

Answers on page 374.

Find the Witness

On Trevalyn Street, there are 5 houses that are identical to each other. You need to gather a witness statement from Henry Riggins, but without any address on the doors you are not sure which house to approach. You know that Riggins lives with his girlfriend and her teenaged son. The staff at the coffee shop around the corner and your own observations give you some clues. From the information given, can you find the right house?

A. The people who live in the house in the middle always help the elderly couple next door, whose children live far away, shovel their walkway.

B. The elderly couple also get help from Matthew and Jonas, who live on the other side of the elderly couple and drive them to the grocery store each week.

C. The couple in house D just put out a stork figurine to celebrate their new baby.

D. One house is vacant while it's being sold.

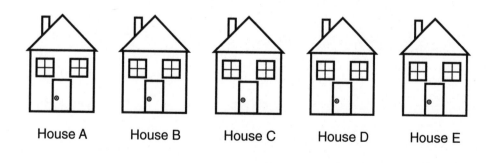

House A   House B   House C   House D   House E

Answer on page 375.

The Car Thief

Litchfield County Police are investigating five classic car thefts which took place over the last two weeks. Each car was a different model and year, and no two cars were stolen from the same town. Using only the clues below, determine each stolen car's production year, model and owner, and determine the town in which each theft took place.

1. The Mustang, the 1978 model and the car stolen from Deerfield had three different owners.

2. The 1972 model year car wasn't stolen from Montclair, Deerfield or Kearney.

3. Of the Mustang and the car stolen from Montclair, one was a 1975 model and the other belonged to Dennis.

4. Thomas has never owned a Camaro.

5. Of Thomas's car and the one stolen from Taunton, one was the 1966 model and the other was the Mustang.

6. Jennifer's car wasn't stolen from Taunton or Deerfield.

7. The car stolen from Deerfield is three years newer than the one stolen from Ridgewood.

8. The Corvette was stolen from Main Street in Kearney.

9. Beatrice's car wasn't a 1969 model, and it wasn't stolen from Montclair.

10. The 1969 model year car is neither the Camaro nor the Continental.

		Models					Owners					Towns			
		Camaro	Continental	Corvette	Mustang	Thunderbird	Beatrice	Dennis	Irving	Jennifer	Thomas	Deerfield	Kearney	Montclair	Ridgewood	Taunton
Years	1966															
	1969															
	1972															
	1975															
	1978															
Towns	Deerfield															
	Kearney															
	Montclair															
	Ridgewood															
	Taunton															
Owners	Beatrice															
	Dennis															
	Irving															
	Jennifer															
	Thomas															

Years	Models	Owners	Towns
1966			
1969			
1972			
1975			
1978			

I Saw Them Wearing A...

The letters in the word BOWLER can be found in boxes 6, 7, 9, 11, 15, and 19, but not necessarily in that order. Similarly, the letters in the other hats listed can be found in the boxes indicated. Your task is to insert all the letters into the grid. If you do this correctly, the name of 1 [more thing] will be revealed in the shaded squares.

Hint: Compare STETSON and STOVEPIPE to get the value of N, then STETSON to DERBY to get the value of E.

Unused letter: Q

BALMORAL 2, 6, 7, 8, 15, 19

BILLYCOCK 6, 12, 15, 17, 19, 24, 25

BOWLER 6, 7, 9, 11, 15, 19

COXCOMB 6, 8, 12, 16, 19

DERBY 7, 9, 17, 19, 22

FEDORA 2, 5, 6, 7, 9, 22

FEZ 5, 9, 14

HELMET 1, 3, 8, 9, 15

HOMBURG 1, 6, 7, 8, 18, 19, 20

JOCKEY CAP 2, 6, 9, 12, 13, 17, 21, 25

PORKPIE 6, 7, 9, 13, 24, 25

STETSON 3, 4, 6, 9, 10

STOVEPIPE 3, 4, 6, 9, 13, 23, 24

YARMULKE 2, 7, 8, 9, 15, 17, 20, 25

1	2	3	4	5	6	7	8	9	10	11	12	13
14	15	16	17	18	19	20	21	22	23	24	25	26
												Q

Answers on page 375.

Track the Fugitive

The investigator is tracking the fugitive's past trips in order to find and recover information that was left behind in five cities. Each city was visited only once. Can you put together the travel timeline, using the information below?

1. Boston was not the third city visited.

2. The fugitive went north along the coastline immediately after visiting San Francisco.

3. Chicago was neither the first nor last city visited.

4. Seattle was visited sometime before Boston, but not immediately before.

5. Miami was visited sometime before Chicago, but not immediately before.

Answer on page 375.

Motel Hideout

A thief hides out in one of the 45 motel rooms listed in the chart below. The motel's in-house detective received a sheet of four clues, signed "The Logical Thief." Using these clues, the detective found the room number within 15 minutes—but by that time, the thief had fled. Can you find the thief's motel room more quickly?

1. The sum of the digits is 2, 4, 6, or 8.

2. One of the digits is larger than 4.

3. The number is prime.

4. If you flip the digits, the resulting number will be greater than 50.

51	52	53	54	55	56	57	58	59
41	42	43	44	45	46	47	48	49
31	32	33	34	35	36	37	38	39
21	22	23	24	25	26	27	28	29
11	12	13	14	15	16	17	18	19

Answer on page 375.

Seen at the Scene (Part I)

Study this picture of the crime scene for 1 minute, then turn the page.

Seen at the Scene
(Part II)

(Do not read this until you have read the previous page!)

1. The placards marking the bullets show these numbers:
   A. 1, 2, 3
   B. 1, 2, 3, 4
   C. 1, 2, 3, 5
   D. 1, 2, 3, 4, 5

2. The police car's front lights were:
   A. On
   B. Off

3. The police car's siren lights were:
   A. On
   B. Off

4. A knife was found at the scene.
   A. Yes
   B. No

Answers on page 375.

Bank Robbery Alert
(Part I)

A local bank was robbed! The bank has a poster up in its lobby, detailing what they know about the robbers. Read the page, then turn the page to answer questions.

Date: November 18, 2020

Time: 4:56 PM

Suspect descriptions:

Suspect #1: 5'8", short brown hair, wearing a mask of George Clooney. Tellers said that the voice seemed female.

Suspect #2: 5'5", short blond hair (dyed with dark roots), wearing a mask of Brad Pitt. Tellers said that the voice could be male or female.

Weapons: Machine guns

Getaway vehicle: motorcycles. Washington state license plates, partial plate N87

Bank Robbery Alert (Part II)

(Do not read this until you have read the previous page!)

Fill in all the information you remember.

Date: _____

Time: _____

Suspect descriptions:

Suspect 1: _____

_____

Suspect 2: _____

_____

Weapons: _____

Getaway vehicle: _____

Answers on page 375.

Quick Crime Quiz

How much do you know about the history of crime scene investigation? Answer the following questions.

1. The first fingerprint classification system was created by a police officer working in this country.
   ____ United States
   ____ Great Britain
   ____ Argentina

2. Do identical twins have identical fingerprints?
   ____ Yes
   ____ No

3. Can someone be born without fingerprints?
   ____ Yes
   ____ No

4. Can you lose or erode fingerprints?
   ____ Yes
   ____ No

5. Can you lift fingerprints from fabric?
   ____ Easily
   ____ Sometimes, but it is difficult
   ____ Never

Answers on page 375.

DNA Sequence

Examine the two images below carefully. Are these sequences a match or not?

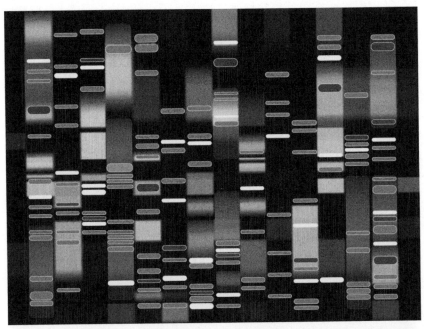

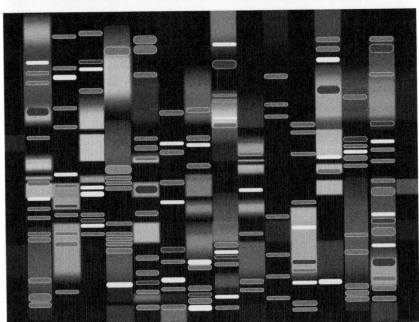

Answer on page 376.

Interception

You've intercepted a message. You think it might be the location of a meeting between two criminals, but it doesn't seem to make sense. Can you decipher the true message?

BANGKOK

ATLANTA

BOSTON

ARKANSAS

OTTAWA

HONDURAS

DOMINICAN REPUBLIC

TRIPOLI

RABAT

PARAGUAY

Answer on page 376.

Detectives

Complete the word search below to reveal a hidden message related to the puzzle's topic. Every word listed below is contained within the group of letters. Words can be found in a straight line horizontally, vertically, or diagonally. They may read either forward or backward. Once you find all the words, you can read the hidden message from the remaining letters, top to bottom, left to right, to find the names of two of the most famous names in detective fiction, and the author who created them.

BANACEK	JIM ROCKFORD
BARETTA	McGEE (Travis)
BARNABY (Jones)	MILLER (Barney)
CANNON	NANCY DREW
DICK TRACY	QUEEN (Ellery)
FRIDAY (Sgt.)	QUINCY
HAMMER (Mike)	SPADE (Sam)
HARDY BOYS	THE HARTS
HERCULE POIROT	THE SAINT

```
        S H E
      S T R A H E H T
    R L O B C E E D A P S
  M I L L E R A F R I D A Y K
  H B J I M R O C K F O R D
  A O L W E K U M T E N
  R E S E T B L S H E E
  N A N R T A E Y E G E
  D A D A D A N P O S C U O
  C B C H Y Q A O B A M Q T O
  Y R A C U C I Y I W
      M N I E R D N A
  T S M A N K O R T
  O N E N C O T A D
    R O Y Y N H L E
```

Leftover letters: _____

Bungled Burglary

We count 17 things that are wrong with this picture. Can you find them?

Answers on page 376.

A Notorious Murder Mystery

Cryptograms are messages in substitution code. Break the code to read the message. For example, THE SMART CAT might become FVO QWGDF JGF if **F** is substituted for **T, V** for **H, O** for **E,** and so on.

CI RAH HNPFW AKSPQ KM GNPZA 9, 1997, CIMF-
SHIRCNF PNL NPRCQR ZAPCQRKLAHP UNFFNZH, NFQK
EIKUI NQ XCJJCH QGNFFQ KP IKRKPCKSQ X.C.J., UNQ
JSIIHB BKUI XW N BPCTH-XW QAKKRHP KSRQCBH RAH
LHRHPQHI NSRKGKRCTH GSQHSG KI UCFQACPH XKS-
FHTNPB. UNFFNZH UNQ NR RAH GSQHSG RK NRRHIB
RAH NMRHP-LNPRW MKP "TCXH" GNJNYCIH'Q QKSF
RPNCI GSQCZ NUNPBQ. NR NPKSIB 12:30 N.G., UNFFN-
ZH FHMR RAH HTHIR UCRA ACQ HIRKSPNJH. UAHI ACQ
THACZFH QRKLLHB NR N PHB FCJAR DSQR 50 WNPBQ
MPKG RAH GSQHSG, N XFNZE ZAHTW CGLNFN LSFFHB
NFKIJQCBH, NIB RAH BPCTHP MCPHB ISGHPKSQ PKSIBQ
MPKG N 9GG LCQRKF, ACRRCIJ RAH 24-WHNP-KFB PNL
QRNP CI RAH ZAHQR. ACQ GSPBHP PHGNCIQ SIQK-
FTHB, NFRAKSJA LFHIRW KM ZKIQLCPNZW RAHKPCHQ
QSPPKSIB ACQ BHNRA.

In Search of Evidence

ACROSS

1. Scottish Gaelic language
5. Kaiser or Maxwell
8. Inflammatory suffix
12. Prison's antithesis, with "the"
14. Fire and fury
15. One of the lab techniques in 26-Across
16. On the authority of
17. Light tan
18. Acqua Di ___ (Armani fragrance)
19. "I'll take that as ___"
20. Piece of copper
21. Highway sign
22. Two-colored ermine
24. CPR giver, perhaps
26. Field of "CSI"
31. "Illmatic" rapper
32. Not those
34. Titled woman
36. Queen of the Nile
39. Start of an Irish flier
40. British rec. giant
41. Rowing gear
42. Digital camera variety, for short
43. Ink impressions that reveal responsibility
46. Boy or girl lead-in
47. Time to vote
48. Critical evaluation
49. Velocity: abbr.
50. Composer of "Dido and Aeneas"

DOWN

2. Rat or squirrel
3. Car option that slides open
4. Terminal datum
5. She turned men to pigs in "The Odyssey"
6. Add decorations
7. Proves false
8. Not online, briefly

9. Evergreen forest of sub arctic lands

10. Start to burn

11. Desert lilies

13. Prism bands

16. Que ___? ("What's going on?")

21. Draw on glass

23. Classy

25. Cell division

27. Former Ford compacts

28. Another name for starfish

29. Hawaii, before 1959: abbr.

30. Heavy silk fabric

33. Generator element

34. Render lean

35. After-dinner freebies

37. Receive with enthusiasm

38. Did the wrong thing

44. Pistol, in old gangster movies

45. Contract to protect trade secrets: abbr.

Motel Hideout

A thief hides out in one of the 45 motel rooms listed in the chart below. The motel's in-house detective received a sheet of four clues, signed "The Logical Thief." Using these clues, the detective found the room number within 15 minutes—but by that time, the thief had fled. Can you find the thief's motel room more quickly?

1. Neither digit is 3.

2. The sum of the digits is either 5, 7, or 10.

3. If the digits were flipped, the resulting number would be found on the chart.

4. The number is prime.

51	52	53	54	55	56	57	58	59
41	42	43	44	45	46	47	48	49
31	32	33	34	35	36	37	38	39
21	22	23	24	25	26	27	28	29
11	12	13	14	15	16	17	18	19

Answer on page 377.

Overheard Information
(Part I)

Read the story below, then turn the page and answer the questions.

An investigator hears a conversation between two criminals, in which one tells the other the passwords to the underground gambling clubs run through his chain of restaurants. He hears, "At the Oakmont location, ask for Leo and tell him, 'Didn't you used to have lemon bars for dessert?' At Golden Circle Plaza, ask for Roger and tell him, 'Say, do you have a cousin named Rhoda?' But Roger's only there Tuesday, Thursday, and Sunday. Don't go to the place on Truman until things cool down, since the cops are watching that location."

Overheard Information (Part II)

(Do not read this until you have read the previous page!)

1. Who is in charge at the Oakmont location?

   _____

2. Where does Roger work?

   _____

3. On what days does Roger work?

   _____

4. What is the password at the Oakmont location?

   _____

Answers on page 377.

Find the Witness

On Webster Street, there are 5 houses that are identical to each other. You need to gather a witness statement from Savannah Jenkins, but without any address on the doors you are not sure which house to approach. You know that Jenkins lives by herself but that she was out walking her dog when she saw the crime. The staff at the coffee shop around the corner and your own observations give you some clues. From the information given, can you find the right house?

A. One barista says she has definitely heard barking from both houses A and C when she walks past them to get to the bus stop. She's not sure about the other houses.

B. Another barista know the single woman who lives in house D has allergies that keep her from owning any pets.

C. The coffee shop's manager says that a retired couple lives in house C. They consider the kids who live in the house next door to them "honorary grandkids."

D. The coffee shop's manager also says that the retired couple on the other side of the family wish the kids wouldn't trek across their lawn to get to the nearby park, but they don't feel comfortable bringing it up to the parents.

House A   House B   House C   House D   House E

Answer on page 377.

Crime Rhymes

Each clue leads to a 2-word answer that rhymes, such as BIG PIG or STABLE TABLE. The numbers in parentheses after the clue give the number of letters in each word. For example, "cookware taken from the oven (3, 3)" would be "hot pot."

1. When investigators are weighing whether to charge someone with a crime, it is said that they (5, 6): _____

2. The burglar who stole food from a variety of summer picnickers was known as the (10, 5): _____

3. The doctor who thought his patient was being poisoned could be said to have a (9, 9): _____

4. The detective who like this sweet wine was known as the (8, 6): _____

5. When the criminal left traces of an adhesive at the scene, it was known as the (4, 4): _____

6. When the captain's second in command seemed suspicious, the detective chose to (11, 5, 4): _____ (the) _____ _____

7. A murder next to a body of water (8, 8): _____

8. A person who wants to be an investigator (11, 9): _____

Answers on page 377.

DNA Sequence

Examine the two images below carefully. Are these sequences a match or not?

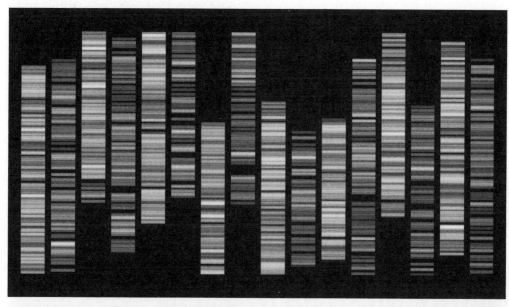

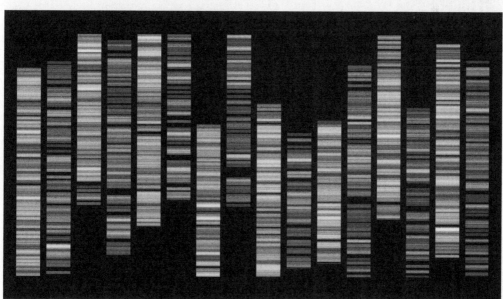

What a Mystery

Every word listed is contained within the group of letters. Words can be found in a straight line horizontally, vertically, or diagonally. They may be read either forward or backward.

ABSTRUSE	INEXPLICABLE
ARCANE	INSCRUTABLE
AMBIGUOUS	MYSTERIOUS
BAFFLING	OBSCURE
CAMOUFLAGED	PERPLEXING
CLASSIFIED	PRIVATE
COVERT	PUZZLING
CRYPTIC	RECONDITE
DISGUISED	SECRET
ENIGMATIC	SHROUDED
ESOTERIC	TENEBROUS
FURTIVE	UNDISCLOSED
HIDDEN	VEILED

```
Y O I D G O B G N I L Z Z U P S V A S
H B R L H I D D E N S V E I L E D O K
C Z S R C N I E C E S O T E R I C V J
L Z U R P S B T I X T E R C E S E M S
A F O S P C F A T P D E J R T Z N I J
S U R G E R T V P L R E C O N D I T E
S R B D R U R I Y I R S Y T F N G Y D
I T E E P T E R R C O U I R I M M X E
F I N S L A V P C A U R Y U P Y A P G
I V E O E B O S X B B T B W B S T T A
E E T L X L C V A L A S D Q V T I A L
D T U C I E V F Q E R B I H I E C M F
F J G S N P F C K V C A S Z H R C B U
C C Y I G L W C U U A Z G E B I L I O
Y P N D I V Z K K U N D U C B O T G M
S Z Y N K H S I R W E K I R I U Z U A
N O G U J O L Q E R U C S B O S J O C
B P W D E D U O R H S B E D J N Q U W
X X L E K F X C J F L D D T D F Q S Y
```

They Fled to Africa

The letters in BOTSWANA can be found in boxes 2, 4, 5, 9, 17, 21, and 24, but not necessarily in that order. Similarly, the letters in all these words can be found in the boxes indicated. Your task is to insert all the letters of the alphabet into the boxes. If you do this correctly, the shaded cells will reveal what ties these words together.

Hint: Compare LIBYA and MALI to get the value of M, then MALI to CHAD to get the value of A.

Unused letter: X

BOTSWANA 2, 4, 5, 9, 17, 21, 24
BURKINA FASO 2, 3, 4, 6, 7, 9, 13, 17, 21, 25
CHAD 1, 10, 17, 18
CONGO 1, 2, 4, 15
DJIBOUTI 2, 3, 5, 7, 14, 18, 21
EGYPT 5, 8, 11, 15, 16
GAMBIA 7, 15, 17, 21, 23
IVORY COAST 1, 2, 5, 6, 7, 9, 11, 17, 19
KENYA 4, 8, 11, 13, 17
LIBYA 7, 11, 17, 21, 22
MALI 7, 17, 22, 23
MOZAMBIQUE 2, 3, 7, 8, 12, 17, 20, 21, 23
UGANDA 3, 4, 15, 17, 18
ZAMBIA 7, 12, 17, 21, 23

1		14	
2		15	
3		16	
4		17	
5		18	
6		19	
7		20	
8		21	
9		22	
10		23	
11		24	
12		25	
13		26	X

Where'd They Go?

You are tracing the route of a criminal. You know he flew from Miami to Seattle, visiting each city once. You also know he chose the cheapest route for the trip. Can you trace the criminal's steps?

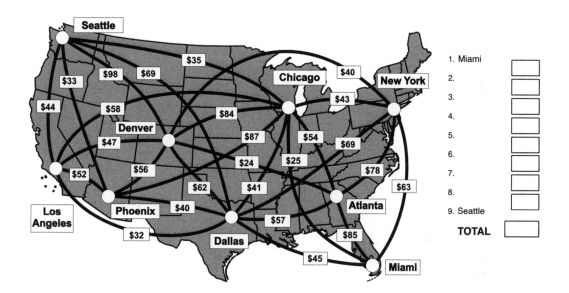

1. Miami
2. ☐
3. ☐
4. ☐
5. ☐
6. ☐
7. ☐
8. ☐
9. Seattle

TOTAL ☐

The Side Door

ACROSS

1. FBI operation which ended up in accusing many wealthy parents
11. Scott of "Diagnosis Murder"
12. Land, as a fish
13. Makes mistakes
14. Pizza slice, usually
15. College admissions bigwig
17. Capital on the Han River
19. File format invented by Eugene Roshal: abbr.
21. Venetian bridge
23. Top of the corp. ladder
24. Fish in a roll
25. Commando rifles
28. Was much easier to pass with Rick Singer's assistance
32. Wedding cake section
33. 2008 French Open champ Ivanovic
34. ___-Turn (sign)
35. Obligations
37. NYC subway line
38. Reeves of "John Wick"
40. 'We want ___!' (baseball chant)
42. An often mildly eccentric and usually elderly fellow
45. Friendly address
47. Majestic dignity
48. Cigarette substances
49. Stanford, Yale and MIT, e.g.

DOWN

1. Crossword clue abbr.
2. A small landing field
3. ____ Bowl Stadium
4. O. Henry twists
5. Private investigator, in slang
6. 'Are we there ___?'
7. Violent explosion

8. Rugby formation

9. Golden Rule word

10. Arctic mammal

11. Cincinnati collegiate athlete

16. War god of Greek mythology

18. Perfect agreement

20. An official in ancient Rome

22. Criminal's fake name

26. Of, or relating to, the highest point reached in the heavens by a celestial body

27. Academic occupations

29. To make smooth

30. Belinda Carlisle "Heaven Is a Place ___"

31. Don Johnson as SFPD In spector Bridges

36. Gentle jab

38. Winslet of "The Reader"

39. Superfood berry

41. 'Tell ___ the judge!'

43. The Theatre Cat in "Cats"

44. PC panic key

46. Med. drama settings

The Shoplifter

Wilbur Jones was arrested this evening on multiple shoplifting charges. He's claiming he's innocent, but there's ample video evidence to make the charges stick. Help the police build their case against him by determining the exact details of his five most recent thefts, each of which took place in a different location and on a different day.

1. Of the jacket and the bracelet, one was stolen on Thursday and the other went missing from a shop on Underhill Road.

2. The five thefts were the one on Sunday, the two at Totopia and Greentail, the jacket, and the incident on Prince Avenue.

3. Of Sunday's theft and the one at Dellmans Department Store, one took place on First Street and the other involved a sapphire bracelet.

4. The incident at Nell Headquarters took place one day before the theft on Underhill Road.

5. Of the Totopia theft and the one that took place on Tuesday, one involved a bottle of French cologne and the other happened on Little Lane.

6. D Street was completely shut down on Wednesday due to a water main break, so we know for sure that no thefts occurred there on that day.

7. The sunglasses weren't stolen from a shop on First Street.

		Items					Stores					Locations				
		bracelet	cologne	drill	jacket	sunglasses	City Shop	Dellmans	Greentail	Nell HQ	Totopia	D St.	First St.	Little Ln.	Prince Ave.	Underhill Rd.
Days	Sunday															
	Monday															
	Tuesday															
	Wednesday															
	Thursday															
Locations	D St.															
	First St.															
	Little Ln.															
	Prince Ave.															
	Underhill Rd.															
Stores	City Shop															
	Dellmans															
	Greentail															
	Nell HQ															
	Totopia															

Days	Items	Stores	Locations
Sunday			
Monday			
Tuesday			
Wednesday			
Thursday			

Answers on page 379.

Identity Parade

Oops! Four mug shots were accidentally sent through the shredder, and Officer Barry is trying to straighten them out. Currently, only one facial feature in each row is in its correct place. Officer Barry knows that:

1. C's eyes are one place to the left of his mouth.

2. B's mouth is not next to C's mouth.

3. A's nose is one place to the left of D's hair.

4. B's eyes are on the same face as A's mouth, and are one place to the right of B's hair.

5. B's nose is one place to the right of his mouth.

   Can you find the correct hair, eyes, nose, and mouth for each suspect?

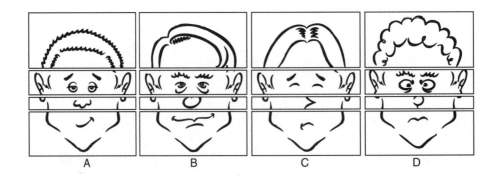

Answer on page 379.

DNA Sequence

Examine the two images below carefully. Are these sequences a match or not?

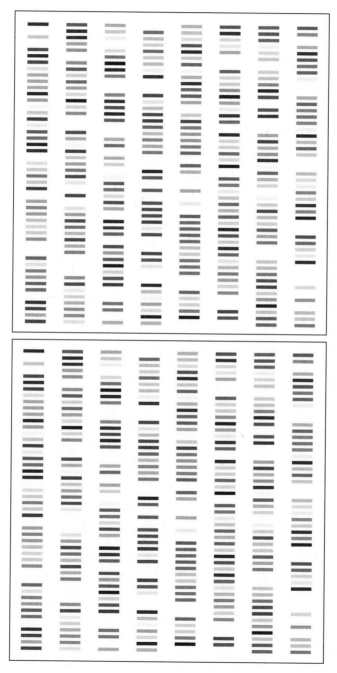

Motel Hideout

A thief hides out in one of the 45 motel rooms listed in the chart below. The motel's in-house detective received a sheet of four clues, signed "The Logical Thief." Using these clues, the detective found the room number within 15 minutes—but by that time, the thief had fled. Can you find the thief's motel room quicker?

1. The second digit is larger than the first by at least 3.

2. Each digit is either a prime number or the number 1.

3. The number itself is not prime.

4. The number can be divided by 3 but not 9.

51	52	53	54	55	56	57	58	59
41	42	43	44	45	46	47	48	49
31	32	33	34	35	36	37	38	39
21	22	23	24	25	26	27	28	29
11	12	13	14	15	16	17	18	19

Answer on page 379.

Code-doku

Solve this puzzle just as you would a sudoku. Use deductive logic to complete the grid so that each row, column, and 3 by 3 box contains the letters from the word POLICEMAN.

		N		I				L
	O	N		L				A
						M		
	A		N		M	L		
		M		I				
E	L		P		C			
M								
P			C		N		E	
I			E		O			

Quick Crime Quiz

How much do you know about the timeline of forensic science? Answer the following questions.

1. A Chinese book from the 13th century, Hsi DuanYu (the Washing Away of Wrongs) described this:

    ____ how to tell drowning from strangulation

    ____ how to tell drowning from natural death

    ____ how to tell heart attack from strangulation

2. The first instance of bullet comparison being used to solve a murder occurred in this century:

    ____ 1600s

    ____ 1700s

    ____ 1800s

    ____ 1900s

3. In the U.S., the first use of DNA evidence to solve a crime occurred in this decade.

    ____ 1970s

    ____ 1980s

    ____ 1990s

4. Scientist Karl Landsteiner established that there were different blood types in this decade.

    ____ 1830s

    ____ 1900s

    ____ 1970s

5. The FBI was founded in this year.

    ____ 1888

    ____ 1908

    ____ 1932

Answers on page 379.

Bank Robbery Alert
(Part I)

A local bank was robbed! The bank has a poster up in its lobby, detailing what they know about the robbers. Read the page, then turn the page to answer questions.

Date: March 3, 2021

Time: 8:55 AM through 9:13 AM

Suspect descriptions:

All suspects were dressed in black, bulky clothes, and wore balaclavas

Suspect #1: 5'9", did not speak, carried a Beretta 92

Suspect #2: 5'10", spoke, presumed male based on voice, carried a Ruger GP100

Suspect #3: 5'11", did not speak, carried a Sig Sauer P365

Suspect #4: 5'8". Suspect 2 at one point said, "Terry (or Terri), get that bag," and Suspect #4 responded. Suspect #4 carried an unidentified handgun

Suspect #5: getaway driver, appeared female with long blonde hair

Getaway vehicle: Honda CRV, model year unknown, license plates unknown

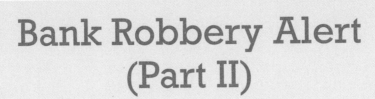

Bank Robbery Alert
(Part II)

(Do not read this until you have read the previous page!)

Fill in all the information you remember.

Date: _____

Time: _____

Suspect descriptions:

Suspect 1: _____
_____

Suspect 2: _____
_____

Suspect 3: _____
_____

Suspect 4: _____
_____

Suspect 5: _____
_____

Getaway vehicle: _____

Answers on pages 379/380.

Help the Detective

The detective is putting together the tools she needs. Can you determine the order of the 6 tools gathered from the information below?

The magnifying glass was one of the first three things gathered.

The notepad was not gathered immediately before or after the pencil, nor was it found last.

The fingerprint kit was found right before the flashlight.

The pencil was found third or fourth.

The magnifying glass was put in the kit, then three other items, and then the measuring tape.

The flashlight was found right before the measuring tape.

Answer on page 380.

Clue

Every word listed is contained within the group of letters. Words can be found in a straight line horizontally, vertically, or diagonally. They may be read either forward or backward.

BALLROOM	LIBRARY
BILLIARD ROOM	LOUNGE
CANDLESTICK	MISS SCARLET
CELLAR	MR. GREEN
COLONEL MUSTARD	MRS. PEACOCK
CONSERVATORY	MRS. WHITE
DAGGER	PROFESSOR PLUM
DINING ROOM	REVOLVER
HALL	ROPE
KITCHEN	STUDY
LEAD PIPE	WRENCH

```
R H C A N D L E S T H K I T C H
O C Y W B I L L I A R D R O O M
P N T Y C A N D L E S T I C K C
M E R D E I L L A R B I L O G M
U R O U L P E L H G B M I L C I
L W P T L D A C R I G C L O G S
P I E S A A D E L O M E N N N S
R M B C R E P L A R O S R E B S
O R S R A L I L S N E M E L A C
S S L M A A P P U R E R H M L A
S W B O R R E Y V R G H U U L R
E H G D U A Y A W R N H C S R L
F I R G C N T R M K U A T T O E
O T L O A O M I B G O L K A I T
R E C F R D R E V O L V E R U K
P K L Y M O O R G N I N I D T D
```

Find the Witness

On Mitchell Street, there are 5 houses that are identical to each other. You need to gather a witness statement from Michelle and Trevor Banks, but without any address on the doors you are not sure which house to approach. You know that the Banks have two teenaged sons. The staff at the coffee shop around the corner and your own observations give you some clues. From the information given, can you find the right house?

A. There are kids at three of the houses.

B. The single dad lives between the vacant house and the bachelor.

C. The single mom likes the big lot she has at the last corner house.

D. The vacant house is not on the corner.

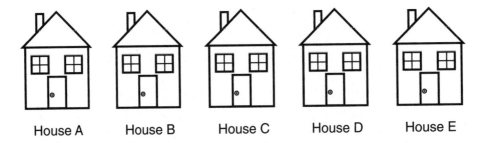

House A   House B   House C   House D   House E

Answer on page 380.

DNA Sequence

Examine the two images below carefully. Are these sequences a match or not?

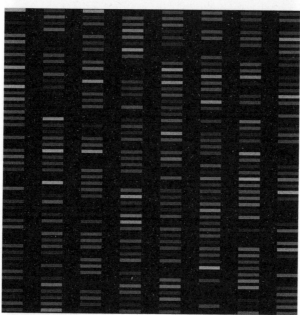

Cipher Trivia

Cryptograms are messages in substitution code. Break the code to read the message. For example, THE SMART CAT might become FVO QWGDF JGF if **F** is substituted for **T, V** for **H, O** for **E,** and so on.

AMXL FSSO GMTLIVW, FSXL WIRHIV ERH VIGIMZIV

YWI XLI WEQI FSSO EW XLI OIC XS XLI GMTLIV. XLI

FMFPI ERH TEVXMGYPEV IHMXMSRW SJ XLI HMGXMS-

REVC EVI WSQIXMQIW YWIH FIGEYWI XLIC LEZI

QERC ASVHW EZEMPEFPI. SXLIV TISTPI QMKLX YWI

E QSVI SFWGYVI FSSO JSV ER IBXVE PECIV SJ WI-

GYVMXC.

Answer on page 380.

Fingerprint Match

Find the matching fingerprint(s). There may be more than one.

A.

B.

C.

D.

E.

F.

G.

H.

I.

J.

K.

L.

M.

N.

O.

P.

Answer(s) on page 380.

Isabella's Missing Collection

ACROSS

1. French forerunner of Impressionism
5. The perpendicular from the center of a regular polygon to one of the sides
11. Ardor
12. Zealous
13. In days gone by
14. It might be proper
15. El ___
16. Head, informally
17. Despite all the efforts, still not found
20. Gallery security worker
21. Legal exam
24. "Buenos ___!"
26. Percussion stick
27. PC monitor spec. of yore
30. Hitch on the run
32. Hawks support it
33. Drowsy
35. Cause for an insurance claim
37. Frozen rain
39. Some finger foods
42. They hang as a theft reminders
46. Vb. form like "to be"
48. In place of
49. Wall-climbing equipment
50. Challenge, legally
51. Carrier to Israel
52. Mini-rage
53. Diatribes
54. Edgar who painted ballerinas

DOWN

1. It's usually returned after ordering
2. Hop or sing ending
3. World's smallest republic
4. Nonet
5. Tel's follower
6. Yearned deeply
7. What fresheners fight
8. Wood shop tool

9. Object of some inflation
10. Crime organization members
12. Of some electrodes
18. Bawled
19. House wing
22. Film's Gardner
23. Netflix's "This Is a Robbery" topic
25. Costa del ___ (Spanish resort area)
26. Romero or Chavez
28. Supermodel Carangi
29. More concise

31. Amount of soup on the stove
34. Elegant tree
36. Like desert vegetation
38. Attendance counter
40. "Honor ___ thieves"
41. Brown shade used in old photos
43. Said 'guilty,' say
44. They're needed for passing
45. Complete collections
47. Rapa ___

Answers on page 381.

Motel Hideout

A thief hides out in one of the 45 motel rooms listed in the chart below. The motel's in-house detective received a sheet of four clues, signed "The Logical Thief." Using these clues, the detective found the room number within 15 minutes—but by that time, the thief had fled. Can you find the thief's motel room quicker?

1. The second digit is more than twice the first digit.

2. The number is not prime.

3. The number is not divisible by 2, 5, or 7.

4. The sum of the digits is 10 or greater.

51	52	53	54	55	56	57	58	59
41	42	43	44	45	46	47	48	49
31	32	33	34	35	36	37	38	39
21	22	23	24	25	26	27	28	29
11	12	13	14	15	16	17	18	19

Answer on page 381.

Overheard Information
(Part I)

Read the story below, then turn the page and answer the questions.

While on a train, a bystander overheard a conversation where one person was giving another the passwords for a set of underground gambling clubs. The bystander heard that the password for the downtown club was, "Do you have the blue cheese burger on the menu tonight?" At the near north location, the password was, "I've been looking forward to the cannoli all night; they never disappoint." At the east side location, the password is, "Are there sunflower seeds in the salad?" At the west side location, the password is, "Can I get the seafood lasagna with broccoli on the side instead of mixed vegetables?"

Overheard Information (Part II)

(Do not read this until you have read the previous page!)

As the undercover investigator charged with going into the clubs, you'll need to know the passwords. How many do you remember?

West side: _____

Downtown: _____

Near north: _____

East side: _____

Answers on page 381.

Code-doku

Solve this puzzle just as you would a sudoku. Use deductive logic to complete the grid so that each row, column, and 3 by 3 box contains the letters from the word SEARCHING.

G	N		H					
		H			E		G	
	A							C
N		S		I				
	C		S		A		R	
			R			S		G
S							A	
	E		R				I	
				C			H	R

Fitting Words

In this miniature crossword, the clues are listed randomly and are numbered for convenience only. It is up to you to figure out the placement of the 9 answers. To help you, we've inserted one letter in the grid, and this is the only occurrence of that letter in the completed puzzle.

Clues

1. Flung

2. Flung

3. Sly

4. Consumer

5. Bad lighting?

6. Was in on

7. Crime _____

8. Seal in one's bathroom

9. Solitary

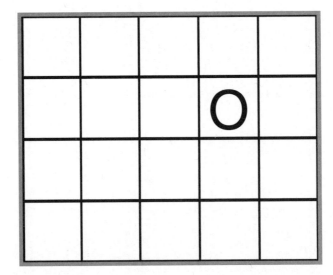

Answers on page 381.

DNA Sequence

Examine the two images below carefully. Are these sequences a match or not?

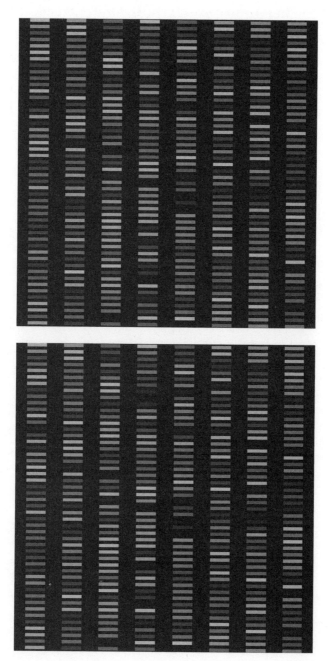

Order in the Court

The letters in ACQUITTAL can be found in boxes 1, 3, 4, 5, 14, 15, and 20, but not necessarily in that order. Similarly, the letters in all these words can be found in the boxes indicated. Your task is to insert all the letters of the alphabet into the boxes. If you do this correctly, the shaded cells will reveal another legal term.

Hint: Compare BAILIFF and PLAINTIFF to get the value of B, then BAILIFF to ACQUITTAL to get the value of F.

ACQUITTAL 1, 3, 4, 5, 14, 15, 20

BAILIFF 3, 4, 5, 17, 21

CASE 4, 6, 7, 20

COURTROOM 1, 2, 12, 14, 18, 20

DOCKET 1, 7, 16, 18, 20, 26

EXECUTION 1, 3, 7, 9, 11, 14, 18, 20

GAVEL 4, 5, 7, 22, 24

HUNG JURY 2, 10, 11, 13, 14, 22, 23

JUDGE 7, 10, 14, 16, 22

LAWYER 2, 4, 5, 7, 13, 25

OBJECTION 1, 3, 7, 10, 11, 17, 18, 20

OYEZ 7, 8, 13, 18

PLAINTIFF 1, 3, 4, 5, 11, 19, 21

VERDICTS 1, 2, 3, 6, 7, 16, 20, 24

1	2	3	4	5	6	7	8	9	10	11	12	13

14	15	16	17	18	19	20	21	22	23	24	25	26

Answers on page 382.

Seen at the Scene (Part I)

Study this picture of the crime scene for 1 minute, then turn the page.

Seen at the Scene
(Part II)

(Do not read this until you have read the previous page!)

1. A wineglass is found on the floor.

   _____ True

   _____ False

2. Both investigators are wearing masks.

   _____ True

   _____ False

3. A chair had been knocked over.

   _____ True

   _____ False

4. A potted plant had been knocked over.

   _____ True

   _____ False

Answers on page 382.

Where'd They Go?

You are tracing the route of a criminal. You know he flew from Miami to Seattle, visiting each city once. You also know he chose the cheapest route for the trip. Can you trace the criminal's steps?

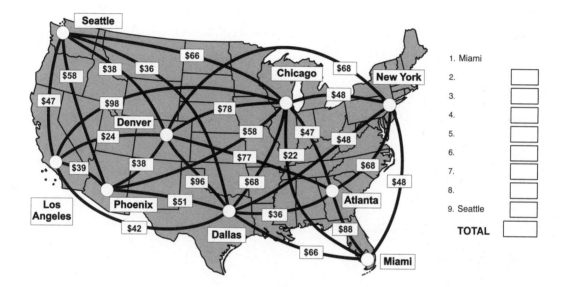

1. Miami

2. ☐

3. ☐

4. ☐

5. ☐

6. ☐

7. ☐

8. ☐

9. Seattle ☐

TOTAL ☐

The Dose Makes the Poison

ACROSS

1. "... even ___ speak"
5. Land of Eyjafjallajökull volcano
12. Life-threatening collapse of the body's essential system
13. Gordievsky, MI6 and KGB spy
14. Given up
15. Via ___ (Rome's "Rodeo Drive")
17. Parker or Waterman
19. Stuff to crunch
21. To grant or obtain an extension of
24. Genetic initials
27. Geometric fig.
29. Quarterback Manning
30. Deadly venom found on the skin of some tropical frogs
32. Caterer's coffeepot
33. One who succeeds

34. Bistro bill
35. Move swiftly
38. Piggy bank feature
40. "If only ___ listened!"
42. Name of eight British kings
45. Chopin e.g.
48. Egyptian goddess
49. Potent killing substance produced by pufferfish
50. "Bitterly unpleasant" life-ending salt
51. Presto

DOWN

2. The undersurface of a foot
3. Small brown singing bird
4. Goaded (with "on")
5. Science associated with computers, informally
6. Corp. money handler
7. Old West lawman Wyatt
8. Big cat hybrid
9. In isolation

10. Whoopi's cover in "Sister Act"

11. Rapper Dr. ___

13. Having too many tasks or activities that require time or attention

16. Reid, Vicky of "American Pie"

18. They're smaller than Queen and King

20. Fatigue symptoms

22. 'You swallow the 50-Across and ___ thing you experience is 12-Across'

23. Charles Lamb's alias

25. DEA agent

26. "___ extra cost!"

28. Eau de ___

31. Walked on

36. Scarlett of literature

37. Mortise mate

39. Between, in poetry

41. Actress Conn of "Grease"

43. A large chunk of Earth

44. Camembert coat

45. Workout target

46. Suffix with complex

47. Grass patch

A Long Path from Crime to Trial

Change just one letter on each line to go from the top word to the bottom word. Do not change the order of the letters. You must have a common English word at each step.

CRIME

_____

_____

_____

_____

_____

_____

_____ sets of two

_____

_____

_____

_____

_____

_____

TRIAL

Answers on page 382.

Overheard Information (Part I)

Read the story below, then turn the page and answer the questions.

A bystander heard two people talking at a coffee shop, only to realize they were counterfeiters! One said to the other, "The order is forty-two $20 dollar bills, fifty $50 bills, and seventy-seven $10 bills. I've left it all in the safe, and the temporary combination is 57-89-10. You need to pick it up by Wednesday at 4 PM or the money is removed."

Overheard Information (Part II)

(Do not read this until you have read the previous page!)

1. How many bills of each denomination are being delivered? (For some, the answer may be zero.)

    $5: _____

    $10: _____

    $20: _____

    $50: _____

    $100: _____

2. What is the combination for the safe?

    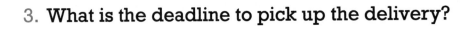

3. What is the deadline to pick up the delivery?

    _____

Answers on page 382.

Find the Witness

On Chicago Avenue, there are 5 houses that are identical to each other. You need to follow up with a witness, Jimmy Perez, but without any address on the doors you are not sure which house to approach. You know that from a previous statement that Perez lives with his husband and has no children. The staff at the corner coffee shop and your own observations give you some clues. From the information given, can you find the right house?

A. One staff member says that Perez drives a compact and his husband has an SUV.

B. They do not have a motorcycle but are interested in buying one, and have said they'll get advice from their next door neighbor.

C. Houses A and E have motorcycles in front of them.

D. House B has a minivan parked in front of it and children's toys in the yard.

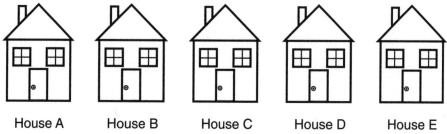

House A   House B   House C   House D   House E

Answer on page 382.

Identity Parade

Oops! Four mugshots accidentally got sent through the shredder, and Officer Wallers is trying to straighten them out. Currently, only one facial feature in each row is in its correct place. Officer Wallers knows that:

1. C's nose is 1 place to the right of her mouth and 2 places to the right of D's hair.

2. C's eyes are 2 places to the left of her hair.

3. A's eyes are 1 place to the right of B's nose and 1 place to the right of D's mouth.

   Can you find the correct hair, eyes, nose, and mouth for each suspect?

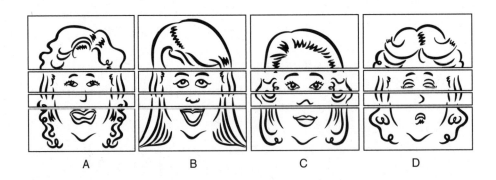

A   B   C   D

Answer on page 383.

Motel Hideout

A thief hides out in one of the 45 motel rooms listed in the chart below. The motel's in-house detective received a sheet of four clues, signed "The Holiday Thief." Using these clues, the detective found the room number within 15 minutes—but by that time, the thief had fled. Can you find the thief's motel room quicker?

1. Of the 2 digits in the room number, one of them is an odd number and the other is even.

2. The second digit in the room number is more than twice as large as the first digit.

3. The room number cannot be evenly divided by 7.

4. If the 2 digits in the room number changed positions, it would still be a room number in the motel as listed in the chart.

51	52	53	54	55	56	57	58	59
41	42	43	44	45	46	47	48	49
31	32	33	34	35	36	37	38	39
21	22	23	24	25	26	27	28	29
11	12	13	14	15	16	17	18	19

Answer on page 383.

DNA Sequence

Examine the two images below carefully. Are these sequences a match or not?

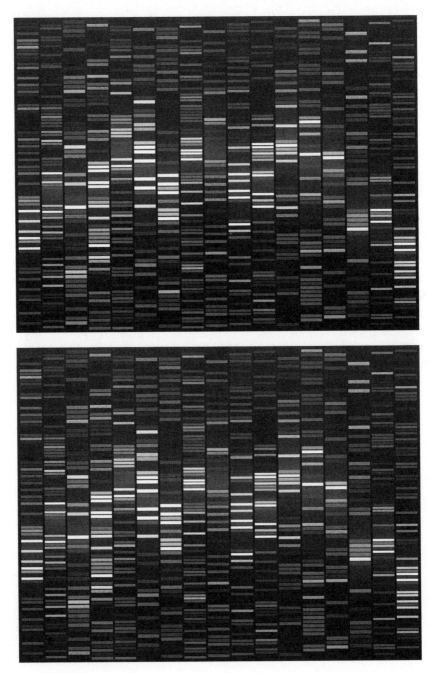

Answer on page 383.

Code-doku

Solve this puzzle just as you would a sudoku. Use deductive logic to complete the grid so that each row, column, and 3 by 3 box contains the letters NO GLUM REV. When you have completed the puzzle, read the shaded squares to reveal a name and 2 words.

Hidden name and words: _____

	N	U	O					
L		G						N
V					N		O	
				G				U
					R	E		
	G	O		M				
R			L	V			U	
		E			O	N		
		L						

The Judge

Judge Penrose ruled on five criminal cases today at the Twelfth Circuit Court. Each case involved a different crime, and none of the five defendants received the same sentence or had the same lawyer. Using only the clues below, determine each defendant's crime and length of sentence (in months), as well as the name of their lawyer.

1. Coretta Colson represented either Rachel or the person convicted of assault.

2. The shoplifter received a longer sentence than Rachel.

3. The perjurer's sentence was twice as long as the one handed down to Bill Barrett's client.

4. Of Nelson and the perjurer, one was represented by Orietta Oswald and the other received an 8-month sentence.

5. Whoever was convicted of identity theft received a sentence that was twice as long as Rachel's.

6. Bill Barrett's client, the person who received the 8-month sentence and Annabelle were three different people.

7. Frederick's sentence was twice as long as that of the person convicted of grand theft.

8. Annabelle was sentenced to 4 months in Wallace County Prison.

9. Nelson's case had nothing to with assault charges.

10. Coretta Colson's client wasn't convicted of grand theft, and Martin McFerry's client wasn't the shoplifter.

		Defendants					Crimes					Lawyers				
		Annabelle	Frederick	Jasmine	Nelson	Rachel	assault	grand theft	ID theft	perjury	shoplifting	Barrett	Colson	McFerry	Oswald	Zimmerman
Sentences	1 month															
	2 months															
	4 months															
	8 months															
	16 months															
Lawyers	Barrett															
	Colson															
	McFerry															
	Oswald															
	Zimmerman															
Crimes	assault															
	grand theft															
	ID theft															
	perjury															
	shoplifting															

Sentences	Defendants	Crimes	Lawyers
1 month			
2 months			
4 months			
8 months			
16 months			

Jewel Thief

ACROSS

1. Change the color scheme or decor
5. Turkey or rooster feather
11. "___ Brockovich" (2000 movie)
12. Central courtyard
13. They give people big heads
14. Celery pieces
15. Light-fingered grandma who has heisted over $2 million in diamonds and jewelry
17. "Saturday Night Fever" music
18. Cut with no bones
21. He stole the tarts of the Queen of Hearts
25. Employ for a purpose
26. First sign of a shark
27. Gunslinger's tally mark
30. Kicks in to the kitty

32. Other, in Paris
34. In the 1970s, 15-Across stole a $500,000 diamond ring in ___
39. Mozart or Beethoven work
40. Commando attack
41. Sets of beliefs
42. Raised, as livestock
43. Non compos mentis
44. Longings

DOWN

1. Hollow-stemmed marsh grass
2. Therefore, in logic
3. In 2015, 15-Across tried to steal Christian ___ earrings valued at $690, but was caught and arrested (again)
4. Kind of football kick
5. Lock fasteners
6. Troop offensive
7. Coloring book necessity

8. Potter's furnace
9. Biblical physician
10. Lifesaving squad: Abbr.
16. Take a load off
18. Kicks, so to speak
19. "Looking for," in personal ads
20. Do-over for Agassi
22. At the back of a boat
23. Be competitive
24. Naval rank below Lieut.
28. Alex Trebek's birthplace
29. Timothy of "Ordinary People"
30. Pendulum path
31. In the vicinity
33. Comb backward
34. Poetic daybreak
35. Small bills
36. Like proverbial hen's teeth
37. Attachment on property
38. Betting stats
39. Chem. or phys.

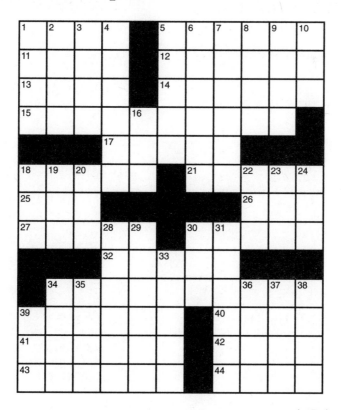

DNA Sequence

Examine the two images below carefully. Are these sequences a match or not?

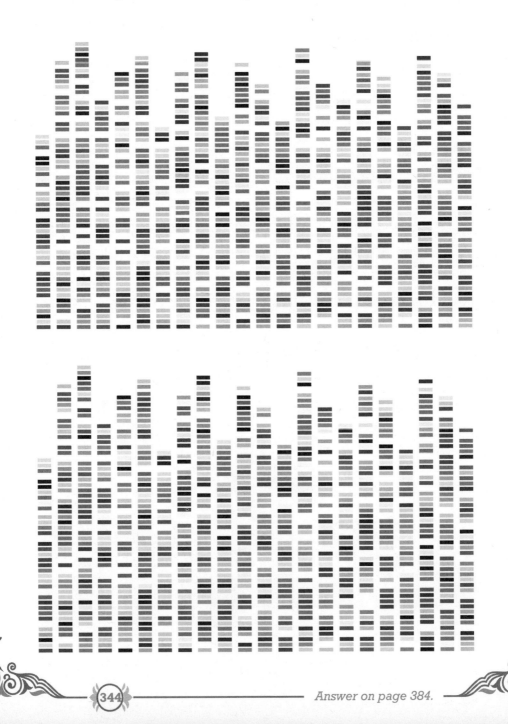

Answer on page 384.

Overheard Information (Part I)

Read the story below, then turn the page and answer the questions.

An investigator hears a conversation where a jewel thief boasts to a friend about her "accomplishments." She says, "You'd be amazed at how many people don't even keep track of their belongings! I went to the Wright party in June 2018, you wouldn't have even recognized me, it was when I had the Trish Bailey ID. I picked up the nicest diamond ring and a set of opal earrings, and they didn't even spot the theft and report it until eleven months later. Imagine having so much jewelry you don't even notice when some goes missing for the better part of a year!"

Overheard Information
(Part II)

(Do not read this until you have read the previous page!)

1. The theft described took place at this party.

   A. Wright
   B. Bailey
   C. Baley
   D. The name is not given.

2. The thief used this alias at the party.

   A. Trish
   B. Patrice
   C. Tricia
   D. Patsy

3. The following items were stolen.

   A. A diamond ring and a set of opal earrings
   B. Diamond earrings and an opal ring
   C. Diamond earrings and an opal necklace
   D. A diamond ring and an opal necklace

4. When was the theft reported?

   A. Immediately
   B. Six months later
   C. Nine months later
   D. Eleven months later

Answers on page 384.

Quick Crime Quiz

How much do you know about the timeline of forensic science? Answer the following questions.

1. If the crime scene technicians did not find a person's fingerprint at the scene of a crime, does that prove they couldn't have been there?

____ Yes

____ No

2. Is "body farm" another word for morgue?

____ Yes

____ No

3. Can a guilty person fool a polygraph test?

____ Yes

____ No

4. Can an innocent person fail a polygraph test?

____ Yes

____ No

5. What does the acronym AFIS stand for?

____ Arson Federal Investigator at the Scene

____ Automated Fingerprint Identification System

____ Automatic Facial Identification System

Answers

Finding a Mole
(page 4)
Answers may vary. FIND, fine, mine, mile, MOLE

Tell a Tale, Go to Jail
(page 4)
Answers may vary. TALE, tall, pall, pail, JAIL

Interception
(page 5)
Take the central letter of each place name and the result is BERLIN.

The Suspect's Escape Route
(page 6)

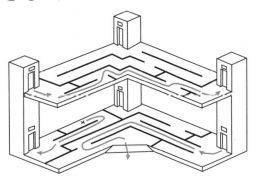

Crime Anagrams
(page 7)
kidnapping; armed robbery; car theft; sabotage; extortion; organized crime; drug trafficking; bombing

Women of Mystery
(pages 8-9)

Track the Fugitive
(page 10)
The order is: Las Vegas, Portland, Montpelier, Pensacola, and Indianapolis

DNA Sequence
(page 11)

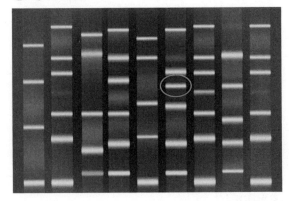

Answers

20th Century Mystery Authors
(pages 12-13)

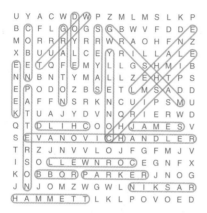

Heist of the 21st Century
(page 14)

What was stolen in the so-called heist of the century? Diamonds, primarily, with some gold and jewelry for good measure. The total came to more than one hundred million dollars. The goods were stolen from the Antwerp World Diamond Centre in Belgium. The thief established himself as a tenant to the building, enabling his access to the vault. He was caught based on a sandwich left near the crime scene. The diamonds, however, were not recovered.

Overheard Information
(pages 15-16)

1. A; 2. A; 3. A; 4. D

Seen at the Scene
(pages 17-18)

1. c; 2. True; 3. a

Motel Hideout
(page 19)

The answer is 38.

Jump on a Train
(page 20)

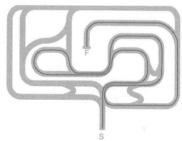

Overheard Information
(pages 21-22)

1. D; 2. B; 3. B; 4. C

Track the Fugitive
(page 23)

The order is: Tokyo, Santiago, Algiers, Berlin, Lisbon

The Museum Robbery
(pages 24-25)

Values	Paintings	Artists	Rooms
$250,000	Sea at Night	Debbie Dale	Bayreux
$500,000	Cape Valley	Alice Ames	Penforth
$1,000,000	May Morning	Elsforth Etz	Russia
$2,000,000	Orpheus II	Cal Carson	Gold
$4,000,000	Blue Elba	Ben Binford	Nixon

Answers

Call the Cops
(pages 26-27)

Crossword answer grid:

```
F L A T F O O T   B M W S
O   N   A   D     I   H
G O T O B E D   I X N A Y
U   I   L   E     D O   A
P I Q U E   S K I D R O W
    U       T     O     A
T H E M A N   S M O K E Y
U       L   D     I
R A W D A T A   T I T U S
N   H   R   Y   I   C   W
R E A L M   G U M S H O E
E   L       L   I   E   E
D R E W   C O L D S N A P
```

Track the Fugitive
(page 28)

The order is: Helsinki, Montreal, Guadalajara, Vancouver, Vienna

DNA Sequence
(page 29)

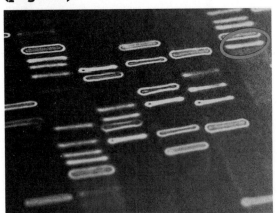

You're Under Arrest
(page 30)

You have the right to remain silent. Anything you say can and will be used against you in a court of law. You have the right to an attorney. If you cannot afford an attorney, one will be provided for you. Do you understand the rights I have just read to you? With these rights in mind, do you wish to speak to me?

Track the Fugitive
(page 31)

The order is: Madrid, Chicago, Bangkok, Singapore, Austin

The Black Dahlia Murder Mystery
(pages 32-33)

Answers

Motel Hideout
(page 34)

The answer is 21.

Open Conundrums
(page 35)

The long-running NBC series "Unsolved Mysteries" profiled more than 1,300 criminal "mysteries" over its 230-episode run. As a result, half the cases featuring wanted fugitives have been solved, more than 100 families have been reunited with lost loved ones, and seven individuals who were wrongly convicted of crimes, have been exonerated and released.

The Suspect's Escape Route
(page 36)

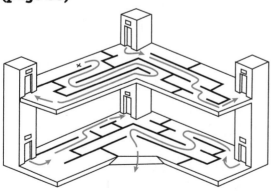

Cold Case
(page 37)

Answers may vary. COLD, hold, hole, home, come, came, CASE

First Steal, then Flee
(page 37)

Answers may vary. STEAL, steel, steep, sleep, sleet, fleet, FLEES

Crime Anagrams
(page 38)

fugitive; captured; menace; post office; apprehended; field office; reward; prosecution

Overheard Information
(pages 39-40)

1. A; 2. D; 3. D; 4. B

Track the Fugitive
(page 41)

The order is: Venice, Bari, Turin, Genoa, Salerno

Robber Riddle
(page 42)

Why did the robber take a bath before going to the bank?
Because he wanted to make sure he had a clean getaway.

Answers

Robber Riddle
(page 42)

Why did the robber wear white gloves?

He didn't want to be caught red-handed.

DNA Sequence
(page 43)

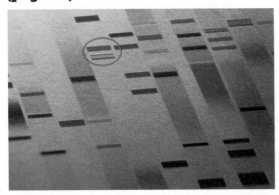

Motel Hideout
(page 44)

The answer is 34.

Track the Fugitive
(page 45)

The order is: Swansea, Liverpool, Sheffield, Glasgow, Manchester

The Serial Arsonist
(pages 46-47)

Dates	Times	Locations	Buildings
March 3	4:45 am	Apple St.	car wash
April 2	2:30 am	First Ave.	surf shop
May 5	1:15 am	Nickel Dr.	pizzeria
June 4	1:45 am	Cranford Ln.	bank
July 1	3:10 am	Twelfth St.	bookstore

Track the Fugitive
(page 48)

The order is: Caracas, Montevideo, Valparaíso, Bogotá, Brasília

In Plain Sight
(page 49)

When you conceal your message in another form of text—for example, hiding information in a grocery list or a classified ad—it is called steganography. Writing a message in invisible ink and writing a regular message over it is one form of steganography.

Jump on a Train
(page 50)

Answers

Interception
(page 51)
Take the first and last letter of each phrase. The meeting will take place "On the tenth of June at noon at the riverbank."

Mystery Terminology
(page 52)

Track the Fugitive
(page 54)
The order is: Barcelona, Osaka, Brussels, Oslo, Munich

Seen at the Scene
(pages 55-56)
Picture 2 is a match.

Motel Hideout
(page 57)
The answer is 17.

Track the Fugitive
(page 58)
The order is: Cairo, Kinshasa, Cape Town, Tripoli, Casablanca

Race to a Solution
(page 59)
After an early career as a jockey, Dick Francis became a mystery novelist. The mysteries in his popular bestselling novels often had a connection to the British racing world.

Spotted at the _____ Store
(page 60)

1	2	3	4	5	6	7	8	9	10	11	12	13
D	I	S	C	O	U	N	T	E	A	J	Y	W
14	15	16	17	18	19	20	21	22	23	24	25	26
Q	L	H	F	B	K	P	R	V	G	M	X	Z

Answers

Overheard Information
(pages 61-62)

1. B; 2. A; 3. D; 4. A

A Lady of Mystery
(page 63)

P.D. James, born Phyllis Dorothy James, was a British crime writer. Her protagonist was police commander Adam Dalgliesh, who also wrote poetry. She was given the title of Baroness later in life.

DNA Sequence
(page 64)

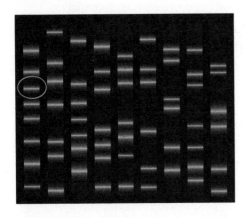

Robber Riddle
(page 65)

Why did the burglar open his sack when it started to rain?
He was hoping for some change in the weather.

Robber Riddle
(page 65)

Why was the thief all wet?
He tried to rob a riverbank.

Motel Hideout
(page 66)

The answer is 13.

Pick Your Poison
(page 67)

From left to right, the bottles are red (1), orange, red (2), pink. The poison is found in the orange bottle.

Baddies of Fiction
(pages 68-69)

L	A	V	A		F	E	N		E	M	I	T
E	V	I	L		L	E	E		P	E	P	A
D	I	E	T		Y	E	W		S	N	O	B
	S	W	E	E	N	E	Y	T	O	D	D	
		R	A	N		E	I	N				
M	I	N	E	R		R	A	J		K	E	G
F	R	E	D	D	Y	K	R	U	E	G	E	R
A	R	T		R	O	O		A	M	B	L	E
		H	U	G		O	N	O				
	N	O	R	M	A	N	B	A	T	E	S	
B	O	N	O		M	E	A		I	M	O	K
S	I	C	S		A	R	M		O	M	N	I
A	R	E	S		T	O	A		N	A	S	A

Answers

Which Sleuth Was He Again?
(page 70)
Humphrey Bogart played the part of both Sam Spade, based on Dashiell Hammett's fictional detective in "The Maltese Falcon," and Philip Marlowe, protagonist of Raymond Chandler's "The Big Sleep."

Motel Hideout
(page 71)
The answer is 27.

Law Enforcement Equipment
(pages 72-73)

The Check Bouncer
(pages 74-75)

Amounts	Dates	Locations	Fake Names
$250	July 30th	Smith St.	Roger Rose
$325	August 12th	Wallace Way	Ned Steel
$400	August 4th	Ball Blvd.	Ted Mobius
$475	August 15th	Lincoln Ln.	Owen Pierce
$550	July 13th	Raptor Rd.	Pedro Hope

Aristocratic Accomplices
(page 76)

1	2	3	4	5	6	7	8	9	10	11	12	13
S	E	N	O	R	I	T	A	Z	D	H	P	Q
14	15	16	17	18	19	20	21	22	23	24	25	26
Y	W	U	L	M	B	F	V	G	C	J	K	X

Methods of Disguise
(page 77)
mustache; hair dye; baseball cap; facial hair; glasses; bandanna; balaclava; beard; makeup; sideburns; umbrella; parasol

Pick Your Poison
(page 78)
From left to right, the bottles are purple, brown, white, yellow, and blue. The poison is found in the brown bottle.

Overheard Information
(pages 79-80)
1. C; 2. C; 3. B; 4. C

Answers

Flee the Scene
(page 81)

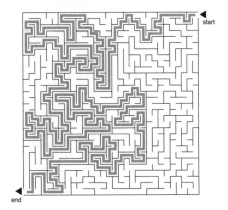

A Mystery from History
(page 82)

The Voynich manuscript is a famous manuscript that has challenged cryptographers. The manuscript supposedly dates back to the early fifteenth century. It contains drawings of plants and other objects accompanied by text, but no one has been able to decipher the text.

Track the Fugitive
(page 83)

The order is: San Antonio, San Diego, Eugene, Houston, Louisville

Interception
(page 84)

Take the first letter of the first word, the second letter of the second word, the third letter of the third word, the fourth letter of the fourth word, and the fifth letter of the fifth word to reveal that the meeting will be held in PARIS.

Seen at the Scene
(pages 85-86)

Picture 3 is a match.

Overheard Information
(pages 87-88)

1. D; 2. A; 3. D; 4. A

Motel Hideout
(page 89)

The thief is in room 36.

More Mystery Terminology
(pages 90-91)

Answers

The Graffiti Gang
(pages 92-93)

Tags	Name	Neighborhood	Colors
15	Lucretia	Uptown	orange & teal
22	Daryl	West Side	gray & purple
29	Patrick	East Side	cyan & silver
36	Clarence	Downtown	green & white
43	Agatha	Midtown	blue & pink

Track the Fugitive
(page 94)
The order is: Indianapolis, Denver, New Orleans, Hartford, Portland

DNA Sequence
(page 95)

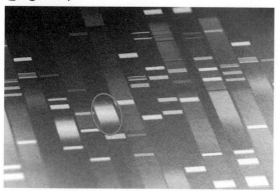

Motel Hideout
(page 96)
The thief is in room 42.

Bank Robbery Alert
(pages 97-98)
1. Suspect #1, female; 2. Small handgun and machine gun with a wood-grain handle; 3. Suspect #2, male, blue stone; 4. Wednesday

Adding Insult to Injury
(page 99)
1994 saw the theft of a version of Edvard Munch's painting "The Scream" from a gallery in Oslo. The thieves left behind a note thanking the museum for poor security. The last laugh was on the museum, though, as police recovered the painting and caught the thieves.

Over, Under, and Out
(page 100)

To the Point
(page 101)
Halberd; spear; javelin; pole arm; harpoon; glaive; naginata; pole axe

Answers

Track the Fugitive
(page 102)
The order is: San Jose, Boston, Charleston, Philadelphia, Omaha

Motel Hideout
(page 103)
The thief is in room 16.

DNA Sequence
(page 104)
They are a match.

AKA: Partner in Crime
(page 105)

1	L	14	U
2	O	15	Y
3	V	16	K
4	E	17	H
5	R	18	B
6	X	19	F
7	S	20	I
8	A	21	N
9	G	22	P
10	C	23	W
11	D	24	J
12	M	25	Q
13	T	26	Z

Police Lineups
(pages 106-107)

A Vendor of Death
(page 108)
Italian poisoner Guilia Tofana lived in the 1600s. She developed a poison called Aqua Tofana and sold it to women looking to murder their husbands. When the police came for her, she fled and sought sanctuary in a church; locals grateful for her previous help protected her. Eventually, however, she was arrested and executed, along with her daughter and several other accomplices.

Answers

Track the Fugitive
(page 109)

The order is: Vancouver, Seattle, Richmond, Toledo, San Diego

Fingerprint Match
(page 110)

J is the matching fingerprint.

Bank Robbery Alert
(pages 111-112)

1. 5'3", fair complexion, heavy New Jersey accent. Brandished a Smith & Wesson 642, never used it. Named "Billy Boy"; 2. Two; 3. Suspect #2, blonde ponytail, eyeglasses, never spoke, shot his gun twice into the ceiling; 4. 17 minutes

Crime Rhymes
(page 113)

1. prehistory mystery; 2. prospective detective; 3. skater investigator; 4. tooth sleuth; 5. gumshoe queue; 6. peppermint print; 7. birder murder; 8. fluoride homicide

Interception
(page 114)

Take the first letter of the first word, the last letter of the second word, the first letter of the third word, and the last letter of the fourth word. Continue, alternating between the first letter of one word and the final letter of the next word, until you have the whole message: Cottage Grove Inn, Room Eight

Seen at the Scene
(pages 115-116)

Picture 4 is a match.

Motel Hideout
(page 117)

The answer is 52.

Criminal Synonyms
(pages 118-119)

```
D A S S A S S I N G S F T N R T
F S A S E A P S E R T S E E H R
F D P H O P L I F T I L H I E C
P I C K P O C K E N G C E G H O
F O R G E R H F O G A R G Y J T
I L Z C R B F S U O E U L S I
B A R R E L R M P L M Z A S A M
U E E E S A S H G L Z D H M U V
R D L L S C B G O E N O K R R D
G G A Z A K U O B A P C D E I R
L U E Z P M T E V L A E D R N E
A R D E S A E O I L R I Y U O D
R D G B E I G F B E R O H M S R
Z N U M R L T R R Y J T L J R U
D A R E T E K C O P K C I P A M
H V D N R R L J F F R E T O O L
```

Answers

Track the Fugitive
(page 120)

The order is: Melbourne, Perth, Adelaide, Canberra (Australia's capital city), Sydney

DNA Sequence
(page 121)

They are a match.

Hostilities of Television
(page 122)

Seeing a murder on television can help work off one's antagonisms. And if you haven't any antagonisms, the commercials will give you some. — Alfred Hitchcock

Bank Robbery Alert
(pages 123-124)

1. Long black hair with purple highlights at the tips; 2. None; 3. Hadleyville; 4. Silver body with red details

They Escaped!
(page 125)

1	2	3	4	5	6	7	8	9	10	11	12	13
S	E	C	T	I	O	N	A	U	Y	M	R	Q
14	15	16	17	18	19	20	21	22	23	24	25	26
B	V	H	F	P	Z	L	W	J	D	K	G	X

The Master Forger
(pages 126-127)

Prices	Titles	Authors	Towns
$325	Dear Deborah	Jen Jonson	Micanopy
$370	At One Time	Gil Grayson	Palatka
$415	Ends & Means	Harry Haupt	West Hills
$460	By the Bay	Pam Powell	Derry
$505	Caught Inside	Nick Nells	Ocala

Building Blueprints
(page 128)

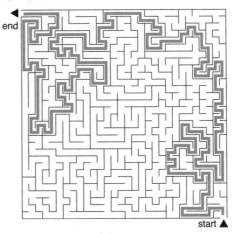

Motel Hideout
(page 129)

The answer is 18.

Track the Fugitive
(page 130)

The order is: Riga, Oslo, Zagreb, Warsaw, Madrid

Fingerprint Match
(page 131)

H is the matching fingerprint.

Answers

Cybercrime
(pages 132-133)

A Murderer in the House
(page 134)

What I feel is that if one has got to have a murder actually happening in one's house, one might as well enjoy it, if you know what I mean. — Agatha Christie, "The Body in the Library"

DNA Sequence
(page 135)

They are a match.

Where'd They Go?
(page 136)

1. Miami
2. Atlanta — 30
3. New York — 33
4. Chicago — 58
5. Los Angeles — 20
6. Denver — 31
7. Dallas — 21
8. Phoenix — 20
9. Seattle — 42

TOTAL — 255

Bank Robbery Alert
(pages 137-138)

1. A; 2. C; 3. B; 4. D

Motel Hideout
(page 139)

The answer is 32.

Track the Fugitive
(page 140)

The order is: La Paz, Panama City, Caracas, Quito, Montevideo

Don't Leave a Print
(page 141)

Answers may vary. LEAVE, heave, heavy, heady, heads, hears, heirs, hairs, pairs, paint, PRINT

Answers

Crime Scene
(pages 142-143)

S	T	A	I	R		S	P	O	R	T
O	U	I	D	A		A	R	M	O	R
D	N	A	E	V	I	D	E	N	C	E
		E	A	R	L		E	S	E	
A	H	A		G	O	Y	A			
L	A	W	M	E	N		M	I	N	T
B	L	O	O	D		F	I	B	E	R
S	O	L	D		M	E	D	I	C	O
		E	G	A	D		S	K	Y	
I	T	S		O	R	E	S			
P	H	O	T	O	G	R	A	P	H	S
S	E	R	I	F		A	R	E	A	S
E	N	E	M	Y		L	A	R	G	E

Jump on a Train
(page 144)

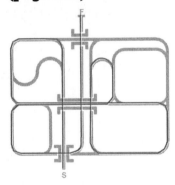

Crime...and Logic
(page 145)

Crime is common. Logic is rare. Therefore it is upon the logic rather than upon the crime that you should dwell. — Sir Arthur Conan Doyle, "The Adventure of the Copper Beeches"

Interception
(page 146)

Take the first two letters of each place name: The meet will take place in "The city of Austin in a big hotel."

Discover the Alias
(page 147)

1	2	3	4	5	6	7	8	9	10	11	12	13
J	X	K	Z	B	S	H	Q	W	F	P	G	U

14	15	16	17	18	19	20	21	22	23	24	25	26
Y	D	V	E	R	O	N	I	C	A	L	T	M

Whodunits
(page 148-149)

Track the Fugitive
(page 150)

The order is: Butte, Cleveland, Des Moines, San Diego, Sacramento

Seen at the Scene
(pages 151-152)

Picture 3 is a match.

Answers

DNA Sequence
(page 153)
They are a match.

Motel Hideout
(page 154)
The answer is 11.

Bank Robbery Alert
(pages 155-156)
1. B; 2. C; 3. C; 4. B

Couldn't You Be More Like Your Namesake?
(page 157)
A young relative of Davy Crockett had the same name as his famous relation, but was an outlaw. He escaped justice in 1872, fleeing to a ranch.

Building Blueprints
(page 158)

Ways to Get Away
(page 159)
run on foot; drive away; train ride; airplane; use a disguise; use an alias; get on a bus; blend in the crowd

Missing Words
(pages 160-161)
1. America's; 2. Justice; 3. Brooklyn; 4. Cagney; 5. Jordan; 6. Diagnosis; 7. Files; 8. Street; 9. Magnum; 10. She Wrote; 11. NYPD; 12. Prime; 13. Rockford; 14. Walker; 15. Trace

```
V B F U C H T Q G U O D S U P
R D Q S T R E E T C Q G I L U
B R E U V H Y F H R J A S D Z
D O P D P Y N S L P X J O U U
A F W K H E H Q R A F O N E T
X K I A M E R I C A S R G R G
M C T K W D M J N B C D A N D
F O L R X E Z G D B Q A I C W
B R O O K L Y N E Z O N D A W
Y T P I B E H W T R A C E A C
E M T L M S Q Q H C B Q L I A
W W M U N G A M P I D K Q L G
E C I T S U J J Z J E S U W N
R F I L E S P W A R R Z D H E
C L S C G T M Z B K H F H P Y
```

The Ponzi Schemers
(pages 162-163)

Years	Assets	Headquarters	Hedge Funds
2007	$50 million	Chicago	Alpha Sky
2010	$32 million	Los Angeles	Wellspring
2013	$225 million	Seattle	Gemstone
2016	$79 million	Miami	Concorde
2019	$105 million	Dallas	Goldleaf

Answers

Motel Hideout
(page 164)
The answer is 49.

Bank Robbery Alert
(pages 165-166)
1. A; 2. A; 3. D; 4. B

When You Don't Want Your
15 Minutes of Fame
(page 167)
The subject of the very first episode of the television show "America's Most Wanted" in 1988, David James Roberts hid in his apartment for four days after seeing his case profiled on television. Among other crimes, Roberts was convicted of armed robbery and murder.

Where'd They Go?
(page 168)

1. Miami
2. Dallas — 20
3. Atlanta — 44
4. Chicago — 55
5. New York — 41
6. Denver — 28
7. Phoenix — 42
8. Los Angeles — 30
9. Seattle — 44

TOTAL — 304

Fingerprint Match
(page 169)
C, F, and I are matches.

DNA Sequence
(page 170)

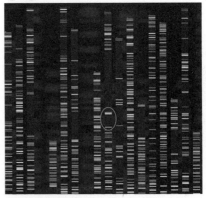

Motel Hideout
(page 171)
The answer is 16.

A Crime By Another Name
(pages 172-173)

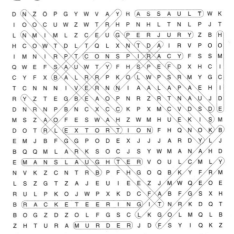

Answers

The Murderer's Itinerary
(page 174)

1	2	3	4	5	6	7	8	9	10	11	12	13
S	A	N	D	I	E	G	O	X	K	U	B	P

14	15	16	17	18	19	20	21	22	23	24	25	26
R	C	Z	M	W	T	H	F	V	L	Y	J	Q

Escape from the Park
(page 175)

Find the Criminal
(page 176)

Answers may vary. LOOK, hook, hood, food, fond, FIND.

Goes Free
(page 176)

Answers may vary. GOES, foes, fees, feet, fret, FREE.

Interception
(page 177)

Take the first letter of the first word, the last letter of the second word, the first letter of the third word, and the last letter of the fourth word. Continue, alternating between the first letter of one word and the final letter of the next word, until you have the whole message: April third, noon, park, Main Street

Catch the Suspect
(page 178)

START

FINISH

Most Wanted Stats
(page 179)

More than 500 people have been included on the list. While more than 90 percent of those listed have been caught, only about 160 were caught because of tips from the public.

Answers

They Played Sherlock
(pages 180-181)

B	A	S	I	L		A	L	O	F	T
A	L	O	N	E		L	E	V	E	R
S	T	U	N	G		B	I	E	R	E
S	E	L		E	V	E		R	R	S
O	R	S	O	N	W	E	L	L	E	S
		B	D	S		A	I	L	E	
C	O	R	E	S		D	U	E	L	S
A	P	E	S		F	O	R			
P	E	T	E	R	O	T	O	O	L	E
E	R	I		H	E	E		C	U	L
E	A	R	L	Y		D	I	C	E	R
S	T	E	A	M		O	F	A	G	E
H	E	S	S	E		N	I	M	O	Y

Track the Fugitive
(page 182)

The order is: Seoul, Dodoma, Skopje, Riyadh, Stockholm

DNA Sequence
(page 183)

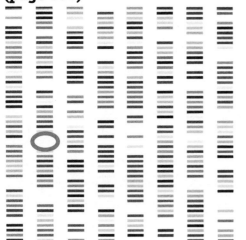

Pinched Paintings
(pages 184-185)

Crime Rhymes
(page 186)

1. stolen colon; 2. yuletide homicide; 3. subliminal criminal; 4. indict knight; 5. swaps cops; 6. steal oatmeal; 7. illegal beagle; 8. mime crime

Overheard Information
(pages 187-188)

1. B; 2. B; 3. A; 4. A

Seen at the Scene
(pages 189-190)

Picture 2 is a match.

Motel Hideout
(page 191)

The answer is 29.

Answers

Mysterious Motive
(page 192)

"What is the meaning of it, Watson?" said Holmes solemnly as he laid down the paper. "What object is served by this circle of misery and violence and fear? It must tend to some end, or else our universe is ruled by chance, which is unthinkable. But what end? There is the great standing perennial problem to which human reason is as far from an answer as ever."

—The Adventure of the Cardboard Box

Bank Robbery Alert
(pages 193-194)

Date: October 15, 2020; Time: 9:45 AM; Suspect description: Male, 6'1", race unknown, hair and eye color unknown; Wore blue vinyl gloves and a mask with red wig and a red mustache and beard attached; Weapon: Ruger LCP II; Getaway vehicle: rust-colored mid-size four-door sedan, possibly a Toyota, model unknown; License plates: Michigan plates, partial number 346 (final three digits)

Track the Fugitive
(page 195)

The order is: Moscow, Tunis, Athens, Brussels, Ankara

The Dognapper
(pages 196-197)

Days	Breeds	Dogs	Families
Monday	Pomeranian	Terry	McHale
Tuesday	Rottweiler	Kenzie	Albertson
Wednesday	Great Dane	Lucille	Voigt
Thursday	Chihuahua	Benji	Singh
Friday	Bulldog	Fido	Jenkins

Stolen Art
(pages 198-199)

Track the Fugitive
(page 200)

The order is: Paris, Vienna, Stockholm, Vaduz, Berlin

Answers

Fleeing Footwear
(page 201)

1	2	3	4	5	6	7	8	9	10	11	12	13
C	L	O	G	S	A	I	X	N	R	P	B	F

14	15	16	17	18	19	20	21	22	23	24	25	26
K	H	E	M	U	V	Z	W	T	D	Y	J	Q

Name the Novel
(page 202)

In "The Murder of Roger Ackroyd," the fiancee of Roger Ackroyd, the widowed Mrs. Ferrars, commits suicide. Ackroyd tells Dr. James Sheppard (the novel's narrator) that she sent him a suicide note in the mail. Sheppard is later called when Ackroyd is murdered. Hercule Poirot is asked to come out of retirement to investigate the crime.

Bonus: Dr. James Sheppard is the novel's narrator, Poirot's assistant, and the murderer.

Track the Fugitive
(page 203)

The order is: Dallas, Denver, Portland, Austin, Nashville

Forensic Careers
(pages 204-205)

Motel Hideout
(page 206)

The thief is in room 34.

Interception
(page 207)

Take the second letter of each word to reveal: Barcelona

Fingerprint Match
(page 208)

The matching pairs are: A and M; B and G; C and P; D and K; E and J; F and O; H and I; L and N

Find the Witness
(page 209)

Chin lives in house D.

Answers

Where'd They Go?
(page 210)

1. Miami		
2. Dallas	50	
3. New York	27	
4. Chicago	35	
5. Atlanta	32	
6. Denver	28	
7. Los Angeles	27	
8. Phoenix	41	
9. Seattle	21	
TOTAL	261	

Overheard Information
(pages 211-212)
1. A; 2. D; 3. D; 4. B

We Still Don't Know Who Done It
(page 213)
One famous unsolved case involves thefts of artwork from the Isabella Stewart Gartner Museum. In 1990, men posing as police officers stole 13 works of art worth hundreds of millions of dollars. Empty frames at the museum show where the artwork was.

Track the Fugitive
(page 214)
The order is: Lima, Buenos Aires, Santiago, Quito, Rio de Janeiro

Crime Rhymes
(page 215)
1. eel steal; 2. bleu clue; 3. beef thief; 4. lime crime; 5. aperitif thief; 6. yacht plot; 7. reflective detective; 8. mint print

Motel Hideout
(page 216)
The thief is in room 22.

Famous Detective Scramble
(page 217)
1. Sherlock Holmes, E. Arthur Conan Doyle; 2. Miss Marple, C., Agatha Christie; 3. C. Auguste Dupin, D. Edgar Allan Poe; 4. Nero Wolfe, A. Rex Stout; 5. Kinsey Millhone, B. Sue Grafton

Track the Fugitive
(page 218)
The order is: Cardiff, Bath, York, Edinburgh, London

Seen at the Scene
(pages 219-220)
Picture 3 is a match.

Answers

Track the Fugitive
(page 221)

The order is: Rome, Milan, Naples, Palermo, Florence

The Wife Poisoner
(pages 222-223)

Years	Wives	Countries	Poisons
1993	Hermione	Canada	hemlock
1999	Corinne	Mexico	cyanide
2005	Annika	Poland	arsenic
2011	Lillith	New Zealand	nightshade
2017	Rebecca	Austria	strychnine

Investigative Tools
(pages 224-225)

```
E S S T P F H A P A P E R B A G S
P Y L H S G V Y K M L R M B C S M
A V A G T E C B I O E O S C E G R
T A I I I G R X R E A T V P S A O
G C R L K O L A H K S N U L V B F
N B E H T R O O L I R I B A G D H
I E T S N S N B G F E A A S J R C
R K A A I E L R B P Z P R T I A R
U L M G R I K U P I E Y R I K Z A
S A G F P T E L S Z E A I C B A E
A H N C T O C E B J W R C B I H S
E C I A N O H R N G T P A A N O O
M G T M E B G L O V E S D G D I T
F A S E T G T A T J I Q E G L B T
S G A R A V L R E G P R T I E V N
S X C A L R L Q B A X Z A E P Z E
R T Y V K H F T O T M B P S A J S
A G E B V T I S O U U K E B P W N
G I C M V D H E K G K H U J E E O
R E D R O C E R O I D U A P R A C
```

The Death of the Party
(page 226)

1	2	3	4	5	6	7	8	9	10	11	12	13
C	O	R	S	A	G	E	Z	I	B	D	F	H
14	**15**	**16**	**17**	**18**	**19**	**20**	**21**	**22**	**23**	**24**	**25**	**26**
K	T	Y	W	P	Q	L	N	U	V	M	J	X

Track the Fugitive
(page 227)

The order is: Barcelona, Los Angeles, Seoul, Tokyo, New York

Find the Witness
(page 228)

Boyd lives in house C.

Motel Hideout
(page 229)

The thief is in room 15.

Quick Crime Quiz
(page 230)

1. True. Fingerprints were used as signatures as far back as ancient Babylon; 2. Fingerprints; 3. True. Bertillion's system produced a set of measurements for each person (for instance, the length of their head, their middle finger, and their foot) that were, in theory, unique to that person. 4. Mug shots; 5. 1850

Track the Fugitive
(page 231)

The order is: Cape Town, Pretoria, Dakar, Gabarone, Nairobi

Answers

Identity Parade
(page 232)

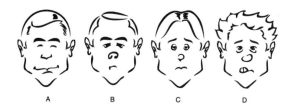

Overheard Information
(pages 233-234)

1. A; 2. B; 3. C; 4; A

Where'd They Go?
(page 235)

1. Miami	33
2. Chicago	45
3. New York	45
4. Dallas	25
5. Atlanta	63
6. Denver	58
7. Los Angeles	87
8. Phoenix	32
9. Seattle	
TOTAL	388

NYSE Evil Sorcerer
(pages 236-237)

The Usual Suspects
(pages 238-239)

Track the Fugitive
(page 240)

The order is: Copenhagen, Toronto, Mexico City, Ottawa, Oslo

Answers

Motel Hideout
(page 241)
The thief is in room 56.

On the Culprit's Trail
(pages 242-243)

The Embezzler
(pages 244-245)

Amounts	Companies	Locations	Industries
$500,000	Melcisco	Atlanta	web hosting
$1,000,000	Wexica Inc.	Chicago	telephony
$2,000,000	Truetel	New York	mobile apps
$4,000,000	Dynacorp	Portland	logistics
$8,000,000	Centrafour	Boston	microchips

Fictional Medical Examiners
(pages 246-247)

Describe the Criminal's Hairdo
(page 248)

1	2	3	4	5	6	7	8	9	10	11	12	13
P	L	A	I	T	S	K	E	R	U	Z	O	M

14	15	16	17	18	19	20	21	22	23	24	25	26
B	F	C	H	N	V	G	D	W	Y	J	Q	X

Bank Robbery Alert
(pages 249-250)
Date: January 8, 2021; Time: 2:17 to 2:33 PM; Suspect description: White male, 5'10", short brown hair, eye color unknown, wore a mask over the lower part of his face; White

Answers

female, 5'5", shoulder-length layered brown hair, eye color unknown, wore sunglasses and a mask over the lower part of her face; A third suspect, description unknown, drove the getaway vehicle. Names: Male robber referred to woman as "Darling," and "Sweet Lily"; Weapons: Machine guns; Getaway vehicle: small-size SUV, black, license plates unknown

Track the Fugitive
(page 251)
The order is: Atlanta, Milwaukee, Tampa, Pittsburgh, Chicago

Motel Hideout
(page 252)
The thief is in room 44.

Seen at the Scene
(pages 253-254)
Picture 4 is a match.

Find the Witness
(page 255)
Patel is in house B.

Track the Fugitive
(page 256)
The order is: Jakarta, Perth, Johannesburg, Rio de Janeiro, New York

Overheard Information
(pages 257-258)
1. B; 2. C; 3. A; 4. A

Motel Hideout
(page 259)
The thief is in room 57.

Deadly Perfume
(pages 260-261)

Answers

Crime Rhymes
(page 262)

1. Fry alibi; 2. lyre fire; 3. steeplechase case; 4. melon felon; 5. knock hemlock; 6. supplied cyanide; 7. gem mayhem; 8. mortician suspicion

Come Together
(page 263)

SUSPECTED

EXAMINERS

BALLISTIC

Codes and Ciphers
(pages 264-265)

Identity Parade
(page 266)

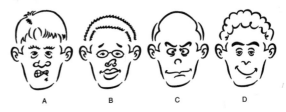

Track the Fugitive
(page 267)

The order is: Seoul, Buenos Aires, Cairo, Paris, Prague

Where'd They Go?
(page 268)

1. Miami
2. Dallas — 38
3. Chicago — 42
4. Atlanta — 38
5. New York — 22
6. Denver — 60
7. Los Angeles — 34
8. Phoenix — 42
9. Seattle — 22
TOTAL — 298

Overheard Information
(pages 269-270)

1. A; 2. C; 3. B; 4. A

Answers

Find the Witness
(page 271)
Riggins lives in house C.

The Car Thief
(pages 272-273)

Years	Models	Owners	Towns
1966	Continental	Thomas	Ridgewood
1969	Thunderbird	Irving	Deerfield
1972	Mustang	Dennis	Taunton
1975	Camaro	Jennifer	Montclair
1978	Corvette	Beatrice	Kearney

I Saw Them Wearing A...
(page 274)

1	2	3	4	5	6	7	8	9	10	11	12	13
H	A	T	S	F	O	R	M	E	N	W	C	P

14	15	16	17	18	19	20	21	22	23	24	25	26
Z	L	X	Y	G	B	U	J	D	V	I	K	Q

Track the Fugitive
(page 275)
The order is: Miami, San Francisco, Seattle, Chicago, Boston

Motel Hideout
(page 276)
The thief is in room 17.

Seen at the Scene
(pages 277-278)
1. C. 1, 2, 3, 5; 2. A. On; 3. Off; 4. B. No

Bank Robbery Alert
(pages 279-280)
Date: November 18, 2020; Time: 4:56 PM; Suspect descriptions: Suspect #1: 5'8", short brown hair, wearing a mask of George Clooney. Tellers said that the voice seemed female. Suspect #2: 5'5", short blond hair (dyed with dark roots), wearing a mask of Brad Pitt. Tellers said that the voice could be male or female. Weapons: Machine guns. Getaway vehicle: motorcycles. Washington state license plates, partial plate N87

Quick Crime Quiz
(page 281)
1. Juan Vucetich of Argentina created the first fingerprint classification system for police. 2. No. 3. Yes. It is rare, but it does happen. 4. Yes. Wear, certain chemicals, and certain chemotherapy drugs can erode fingerprints, but it is difficult to do. 5. Researchers have been developing techniques to lift fingerprints off fabric, but it is more difficult than lifting them from other materials.

Answers

DNA Sequence
(page 282)

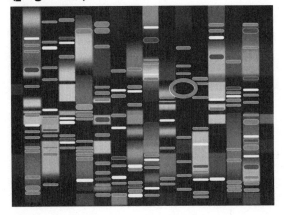

Interception
(page 283)

Take the last letter of each place name to reveal: Kansas City

Detectives
(pages 284-285)

The leftover letters spell: Sherlock Holmes and Doctor Watson (Doyle).

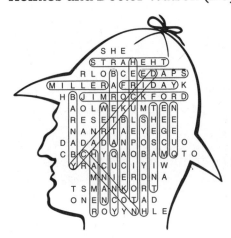

Bungled Burglary
(page 286)

1. woman coming out of painting; 2. glass of water sitting on edge of window; 3. curtains don't match; 4. fish out of water; 5. thief has Santa hat; 6. thief has one bare foot; 7. dresser has zippers instead of knobs; 8. thief brought gifts; 9. bulldog has cat tail; 10. flowers have no stems into vase; 11. drawers hanging in mid-air; 12. Tiny's bowl is a hat; 13. screwdriver instead of knitting needle; 14. ball of yarn turns into a snake; 15. chair's arms turn into teddy bear feet; 16. slippers and socks attached to no one; 17. weeds growing in room

A Notorious Murder Mystery
(page 287)

In the early hours of March 9, 1997, influential rap artist Christopher Wallace, also known as Biggie Smalls or Notorious B.I.G., was gunned down by a drive-by shooter outside the Petersen Automotive Museum on Wilshire Boulevard. Wallace was at the museum to attend the after-party for "Vibe" magazine's Soul Train Music Awards. At around 12:30 A.M., Wallace left the event with his

Answers

entourage. When his vehicle stopped at a red light just 50 yards from the museum, a black Chevy Impala pulled alongside, and the driver fired numerous rounds from a 9mm pistol, hitting the 24-year-old rap star in the chest. His murder remains unsolved, although plenty of conspiracy theories surround his death.

In Search of Evidence
(pages 288-289)

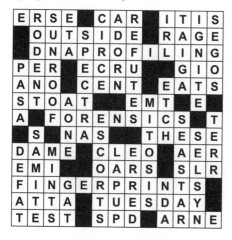

Motel Hideout
(page 290)

The thief is in room 41.

Overheard Information
(pages 291-292)

1. Leo; 2. Golden Circle Plaza; 3. Tuesday, Thursday, and Saturday; 4. Didn't you used to have lemon bars for dessert?

Find the Witness
(page 293)

Jenkins lives in house E.

Crime Rhymes
(page 294)

1. might indict; 2. watermelon felon; 3. physician suspicion; 4. vermouth sleuth; 5. glue clue; 6. investigate the first mate; 7. lakeside homicide; 8. prospective detective

DNA Sequence
(page 295)

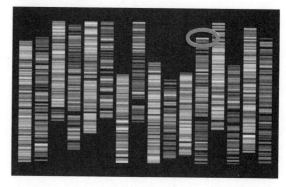

Answers

What a Mystery
(pages 296-297)

```
Y O I D G O B G N I L Z Z U P S V A S
H B R L H I D D E N S V E I L E D O K
C Z S R C N I E C E S O T E R I C V J
L Z U R P S B T I X T E R C E S E M S
A F O S P C F A T P D E J R T Z N I J
S U R G E R T V P L R E C O N D I T E
S R B D R U R I Y I R S Y T F N G Y D
I T E E P T E R R C O U I R I M M X E
F I N S L A V P C A U R Y U P Y A P G
I V E O E B O S X B B T B W B S T T A
E E T L X L C V A L A S D Q V T I A L
D T U C I E V F Q E R B I H I E C M F
F J G S N P F C K V C A S Z H R C B U
C C Y I G L W C U U A Z G E B I L I O
Y P N D V Z K K U N D U C B O T G M A
S Z Y N K H S I R W E K I R I U Z U O
N O G U J O L Q E R U C S B O S J O C
B P W D E D U O R H S B E D J N Q U W
X X L E K F X C J F L D D T D F Q S Y
```

Where'd They Go?
(page 299)

1. Miami — 25
2. Chicago — 43
3. New York — 69
4. Dallas — 57
5. Atlanta — 24
6. Denver — 47
7. Los Angeles — 52
8. Phoenix — 33
9. Seattle

TOTAL — 350

They Fled to Africa
(page 298)

#	Letter	#	Letter
1	C	14	J
2	O	15	G
3	U	16	P
4	N	17	A
5	T	18	D
6	R	19	V
7	I	20	Q
8	E	21	B
9	S	22	L
10	H	23	M
11	Y	24	W
12	Z	25	F
13	K	26	X

The Side Door
(pages 300-301)

```
■ V A R S I T Y B L U E S ■
B A I O ■ R E E L I N ■ E
E R R S ■ O C T A N T ■ A
A ■ D E A N ■ ■ S E O U L
R A R ■ R I A L T O ■ N ■
C E O ■ E E L ■ ■ U Z I S
A D M I S S I O N T E S T
T I E R ■ ■ A N A ■ N O U
■ L ■ O N U S E S ■ I N D
K E A N U ■ ■ A H I T ■ I
A ■ C O D G E R ■ T H E E
T ■ A U G U S T ■ T A R S
E L I T E S C H O O L S ■
```

Answers

The Shoplifter
(pages 302-303)

Days	Items	Stores	Locations
Sunday	drill	Nell HQ	First St.
Monday	jacket	City Shop	Underhill Rd.
Tuesday	cologne	Greentail	D St.
Wednesday	sunglasses	Totopia	Little Ln.
Thursday	bracelet	Dellmans	Prince Ave.

Identity Parade
(page 304)

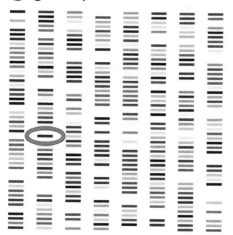

A   B   C   D

DNA Sequence
(page 305)

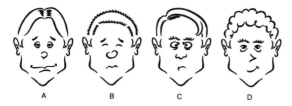

Motel Hideout
(page 306)

The thief is in room 15.

Code-doku
(page 307)

Quick Crime Quiz
(page 308)

1. How to tell drowning from strangulation. 2. 1800s. 3. 1980s. 4. 1900s. 5. 1908.

Bank Robbery Alert
(pages 309-310)

Date: March 3, 2021. Time: 8:55 AM through 9:13 AM. All suspects were dressed in black, bulky clothes, and wore balaclavas. Suspect #1: 5'9", did not speak, carried a Beretta 92. Suspect #2: 5'10", spoke, presumed male based on voice, carried a Ruger GP100. Suspect #3: 5'11", did not speak, carried a Sig Sauer P365. Suspect #4: 5'8". Suspect 2 at one point said, "Terry

Answers

(or Terri), get that bag," and Suspect #4 responded. Suspect #4 carried an unidentified handgun. Suspect #5: getaway driver, appeared female with long blonde hair. Getaway vehicle: Honda CRV, model year unknown, license plates unknown

Help the Detective
(page 311)
The order is: notepad, magnifying glass, pencil, fingerprint kit, flashlight, measuring tape

Clue
(pages 312-313)

Find the Witness
(page 314)
The Banks' live in house A.

DNA Sequence
(page 315)

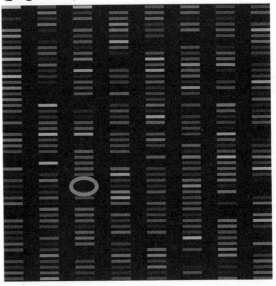

Cipher Trivia
(page 316)
With book ciphers, both sender and receiver use the same book as the key to the cipher. The Bible and particular editions of the dictionary are sometimes used because they have many words available. Other people might use a more obscure book for an extra layer of security.

Fingerprint Match
(page 317)
E is the matching fingerprint.

Answers

Isabella's Missing Collection
(pages 318-319)

M	A	N	E	T		A	P	O	T	H	E	M
E	L	A	N		A	V	I	D		A	G	O
N	O	U	N		N	I	N	O		N	O	B
U	N	R	E	C	O	V	E	R	E	D		S
	G	U	A	R	D		D		L	S	A	T
A		D	I	A	S		C	L	A	V	E	
R	G	B		E	L	O	P	E		W	A	R
T	I	R	E	D		L	O	S	S			S
H	A	I	L		S		T	A	P	A	S	
E		E	M	P	T	Y	F	R	A	M	E	S
I	N	F		L	I	E	U		R	O	P	E
S	U	E		E	L	A	L		S	N	I	T
T	I	R	A	D	E	S		D	E	G	A	S

Motel Hideout
(page 320)

The thief is in room 39.

Overheard Information
(pages 321-322)

West side: "Can I get the seafood lasagna with broccoli on the side instead of mixed vegetables?" Downtown: "Do you have the blue cheese burger on the menu tonight?" Near north: "I've been looking forward to the cannoli all night; they never disappoint." East side: "Are there sunflower seeds in the salad?"

Code-doku
(page 323)

G	N	I	H	C	R	A	E	S
C	S	H	A	N	E	R	G	I
R	A	E	I	G	S	H	N	C
N	R	S	G	I	H	E	C	A
I	C	G	S	E	A	N	R	H
E	H	A	C	R	N	S	I	G
S	G	R	N	H	I	C	A	E
H	E	C	R	A	G	I	S	N
A	I	N	E	S	C	G	H	R

Fitting Words
(page 324)

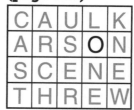

C	A	U	L	K
A	R	S	O	N
S	C	E	N	E
T	H	R	E	W

DNA Sequence
(page 325)

Answers

Order in the Court
(page 326)

1	2	3	4	5	6	7	8	9	10	11	12	13
T	R	I	A	L	S	E	Z	X	J	N	M	Y

14	15	16	17	18	19	20	21	22	23	24	25	26
U	Q	D	B	O	P	C	F	G	H	V	W	K

Seen at the Scene
(pages 327-328)
1. True; 2. False; 3. False; 4. True

Where'd They Go?
(page 329)

1. Miami

2. Chicago	22
3. New York	48
4. Atlanta	68
5. Dallas	36
6. Phoenix	51
7. Los Angeles	39
8. Denver	24
9. Seattle	38
TOTAL	326

The Dose Makes the Poison
(pages 330-331)

A Long Path from Crime to Trial
(page 332)
Answers may vary. CRIME, grime, gripe, grips, grins, gains, pains, pairs, hairs, hairy, dairy, daily, drily, drill, trill, TRIAL

Overheard Information
(pages 333-334)
1. Zero $5 bills; 77 $10 bills; 42 $20 bills; 50 $50 bills, and 0 $100 bills; 2. 57-89-10; 3. Wednesday at 4 PM

Find the Witness
(page 335)
Perez lives in house D.

Answers

Identity Parade
(page 336)

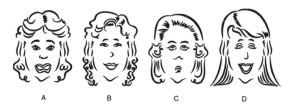

A   B   C   D

Motel Hideout
(page 337)

The thief is in room 25.

DNA Sequence
(page 338)

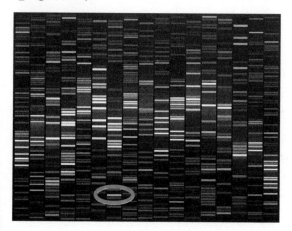

Code-doku
(page 339)

The Judge
(pages 340-341)

Sentences	Defendants	Crimes	Lawyers
1 month	Rachel	grand theft	McFerry
2 months	Frederick	ID theft	Barrett
4 months	Annabelle	perjury	Oswald
8 months	Nelson	shoplifting	Zimmerman
16 months	Jasmine	assault	Colson

Jewel Thief
(pages 342-343)

Answers

DNA Sequence
(page 344)

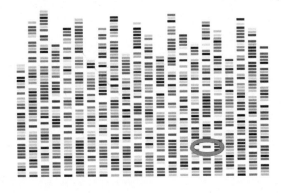

Overheard Information
(pages 345-346)

1. A; 2. A; 3. A; 4. D

Quick Crime Quiz
(page 347)

1. No. They may have been there but worn gloves, for example. 2. No. A body farm describes a place where forensic investigators test to see what happens to corpses under different conditions. 3. Yes. 4. Yes. Many courts do not admit polygraph evidence, because they can show both false negatives and false positives. 5. Automated Fingerprint Identification System